# SINGAPORE
## TRAVEL GUIDE

**SHOPS, RESTAURANTS, ATTRACTIONS & NIGHTLIFE**

The Most Positively
Reviewed and Recommended
by Locals and Travelers

EGP
Editorial

# SINGAPORE

## TRAVEL GUIDE

SHOPS, RESTAURANTS, ATTRACTIONS & NIGHTLIFE

SINGAPORE TRAVEL GUIDE 2022
Shops, Restaurants, Bars & Nightlife

© Rose F. Jones
© E.G.P. Editorial

Printed in USA.

ISBN-13: 9798749360646

# INDEX

## *SINGAPORE TRAVEL GUIDE*

### *Shops, Restaurants, Attractions & Nightlife*

*This directory is dedicated to Singapore Business Owners and Managers
who provide the experience that the locals and tourists enjoy.
Thanks you very much for all that you do and thank for being the "People Choice".*

*Thanks to everyone that posts their reviews online and
the amazing reviews sites that make our life easier.*

*The places listed in this book are the most positively reviewed
and recommended by locals and travelers from around the world.*

*Thank you for your time and enjoy the directory that is
designed with locals and tourist in mind!*

# TOP 200 SHOPS

Recommended by Locals & Trevelers

(From #1 to #200)

#1
## Kinokuniya
Bookstore
**Average price:** Moderate
**District:** Orchard
**Address:** 391 Orchard Road
Singapore 238872 Singapore
**Phone:** +65 6737 5021

#2
## Ion Orchard
Shopping Center
**Average price:** Exclusive
**District:** Orchard
**Address:** 2 Orchard Turn
Singapore 238801 Singapore
**Phone:** +65 6238 8228

#3
## Clarke Quay
Shopping Center
**Average price:** Exclusive
**District:** Clarke Quay
**Address:** 3 River Valley Rd
Singapore 179024 Singapore
**Phone:** +65 6337 3292

#4
## Bugis Street
Shopping Center
**Average price:** Moderate
**District:** Bugis
**Address:** 4 New Bugis Street
Singapore 188868 Singapore
**Phone:** +65 6338 9513

#5
## The Shoppes at Marina Bay Sands
Shopping Center
**Average price:** Exclusive
**District:** Bayfront
**Address:** 2 Bayfront Ave
Singapore 018972 Singapore
**Phone:** +65 6688 7027

#6
## Tekka Market
Farmers Market, Ethnic Food
Shopping Center
**Average price:** Moderate
**District:** Little India
**Address:** #01-201 Buffalo Rd
Singapore 210665 Singapore
**Phone:** +65 6294 4901

#7
## Isetan
Department Store, Grocery
**Average price:** Expensive
**District:** Tanglin
**Address:** 350 Orchard Rd
Singapore 238868 Singapore
**Phone:** +65 6733 1111

#8
## Haw Par Villa
Museums, Art Gallery
**Average price:** Moderate
**District:** Kent Ridge, Pasir Panjang
**Address:** 262 Pasir Panjang Road
Singapore 118628 Singapore
**Phone:** +65 6872 2780

#9
## Artistry
Coffee & Tea, Art Gallery
**Average price:** Expensive
**District:** Arab Street, Lavender
**Address:** 17 Jalan Pinang
Singapore 199149 Singapore
**Phone:** +65 6298 2420

#10
## Carpenter and Cook
Bakeries, Cafe, Home Decor
**Average price:** Expensive
**District:** Upper Bukit Timah
**Address:** 19 Lorong Kilat
Singapore 598120 Singapore
**Phone:** +65 6463 3648

#11
## BooksActually
Bookstore
**Average price:** Expensive
**District:** Tiong Bahru
**Address:** 9 Yong Siak Street
Singapore 168645 Singapore
**Phone:** +65 6222 9195

#12
## Littered With Books
Bookstore
**Average price:** Expensive
**District:** Duxton Hill, Tanjong Pagar
**Address:** 20 Duxton Rd
Singapore 089486 Singapore
**Phone:** +65 6220 6824

#13
## Queensway Shopping Centre
Shopping Center, Sporting Goods
**Average price:** Expensive
**District:** Alexandra
**Address:** 1 Queensway
Singapore 149053 Singapore
**Phone:** +65 6476 1227

#14
## Basheer Graphic Books
Bookstore
**Average price:** Expensive
**District:** Bras Brasah
**Address:** 231 Bain Street
Singapore 180231 Singapore
**Phone:** +65 6336 0810

#15
## Camera Rental Centre
Photographers
**Average price:** Expensive
**District:** Clarke Quay
**Address:** 23 New Bridge Rd
Singapore 059389 Singapore
**Phone:** +65 9650 4158

#16
## DBS Arts Centre
Art Gallery, Cinema, Performing Arts
**Average price:** Moderate
**District:** Robertson Quay
**Address:** 20 Merbau Road
Singapore 239035 Singapore
**Phone:** +65 6733 8166

#17
## Taylor B
Antiques, Furniture Store, Home Decor
**Average price:** Expensive
**District:** Keppel
**Address:** 43 Keppel Road
Singapore 099418 Singapore
**Phone:** +65 6225 7090

#18
## iBrew Marketing
Grocery, Shopping
**Average price:** Expensive
**District:** Clementi
**Address:** Blk 354 Clementi Avenue 2
Singapore 120354 Singapore
**Phone:** +65 6873 3001

#19
## Cat Socrates
Home & Garden, Bookstore
**Average price:** Expensive
**District:** Bugis, Bras Brasah
**Address:** 231 Bain St
Singapore 180231 Singapore
**Phone:** +65 6333 0870

#20
## Uniqlo
Fashion
**Average price:** Moderate
**District:** Orchard
**Address:** 2 Orchard Turn,
#B2-38/#B3-51, 238801 Singapore
**Phone:** +65 6509 1073

#21
## Rockstar by Soon Lee
Fashion
**Average price:** Expensive
**District:** Somerset, Orchard
**Address:** 8 Grange Rd
Singapore 239695 Singapore
**Phone:** +65 6836 8201

#22
## Bugis+
Shopping Center
**Average price:** Expensive
**District:** Bugis
**Address:** 201 Victoria Street
Singapore 188067 Singapore
**Phone:** +65 6634 6810

#23
## Typo
Office Equipment, Cards & Stationery,
Art Supplies
**Average price:** Expensive
**District:** Somerset, Orchard
**Address:** 313 Somerset
Singapore 238895 Singapore
**Phone:** +65 6509 6951

#24
## Daiso
Shopping
**Average price:** Moderate
**District:** Dhoby Ghaut, Orchard
**Address:** 68 Orchard Road
Singapore 238839 Singapore
**Phone:** +65 6884 9210

#25
## Woods in the Books
Comic Books, Bookstore
**Average price:** Expensive
**District:** Ann Siang Hill, Tanjong Pagar
**Address:** 58 Club Street
Singapore 069433 Singapore
**Phone:** +65 6222 9980

#26
## Forever21
Women's Clothing
**Average price:** Expensive
**District:** Orchard
**Address:** 437 Orchard Road
Singapore 238877 Singapore
**Phone:** +65 6887 5443

#27
## Francfranc
Furniture Store, Home Decor
**Average price:** Exclusive
**District:** Harbourfront
**Address:** 1 HarbourFront Walk
Singapore 098585 Singapore
**Phone:** +65 6376 8077

#28
## IKEA
Furniture Store
**Average price:** Expensive
**District:** Tampines
**Address:** 60 Tampines North Drive 2
Singapore 528764 Singapore
**Phone:** +65 6786 6868

#29
## Sephora
Cosmetics & Beauty Supply
**Average price:** Expensive
**District:** Orchard
**Address:** 2 Orchard Turn
Singapore 238801 Singapore
**Phone:** +65 6509 8255

#30
## Tampines 1
Shopping Center
**Average price:** Exclusive
**District:** Tampines
**Address:** 10 Tampines Central 1
Singapore 529536 Singapore
**Phone:** +65 6572 5500

#31
## Marks & Spencer
Department Store
**Average price:** Expensive
**District:** Tanglin
**Address:** 501 Orchard Road
Singapore 238880 Singapore
**Phone:** +65 6733 8122

#32
## Sia Huat
Kitchen & Bath, Wholesale Store
**Average price:** Expensive
**District:** Chinatown
**Address:** 7 Temple Street
Singapore 058560 Singapore
**Phone:** +65 6223 1732

#33
## The Olde Cuban
Tobacco Shops
**Average price:** Exclusive
**District:** Chinatown
**Address:** 2 Trengganu Street
Singapore 058456 Singapore
**Phone:** +65 6222 2207

#34
## Uniqlo
Fashion
**Average price:** Moderate
**District:** Bugis
**Address:** 201 Victoria Street
Singapore 188067 Singapore
**Phone:** +65 6238 7401

#35
## Dustbunny Vintage
Used, Vintage & Consignment
**Average price:** Expensive
**District:** Telok Blangah
**Address:** BLk 112 #01-203 Bukit
Purmei Road, 090112 Singapore
**Phone:** +65 6274 4200

#36
## Wood Would
Bookstore, Cards & Stationery
**Average price:** Exclusive
**District:** Somerset, Orchard
**Address:** 333A Orchard Road
Singapore 238897 Singapore
**Phone:** +65 6735 6136

#37
## Qisahn
Videos & Video Game Rental,
Computers
**Average price:** Expensive
**District:** Tanglin
**Address:** 545 Orchard Rd Far East
Shopping Centre
Singapore 238882 Singapore
**Phone:** +65 3110 3518

#38
## Select Books Pte Ltd
Bookstore
**Average price:** Moderate
**District:** Novena
**Address:** 65A Jalan Tenteram
Singapore 328958 Singapore
**Phone:** +65 6251 3798

#39
## Plaza Singapura
Shopping Center
**Average price:** Expensive
**District:** Dhoby Ghaut, Orchard
**Address:** 68 Orchard Road
Singapore 238839 Singapore
**Phone:** +65 6513 3585

#40
## Sim Lim Square
Shopping Center
**Average price:** Expensive
**District:** Bencoolen
**Address:** 1 Rochor Canal Road
Singapore 188504 Singapore
**Phone:** +65 6338 3859

#41
## Singapore Art Museum
Art Gallery
**Average price:** Expensive
**District:** Bencoolen, Bras Brasah
**Address:** 71 Bras Basah Road
Singapore 189555 Singapore
**Phone:** +65 6332 3222

#42
## Jaben Network
Electronics
**Average price:** Moderate
**District:** City Hall
**Address:** 1 Coleman St
Singapore 179803 Singapore
**Phone:** +65 6338 3369

#43
**PaperMarket**
Cards & Stationery
**Average price:** Expensive
**District:** Dhoby Ghaut, Orchard
**Address:** 68 Orchard Road
Singapore 238839 Singapore
**Phone:** +65 6333 9002

#44
**The Substation**
Performing Arts, Cinema, Art Gallery
**Average price:** Moderate
**District:** Bras Brasah, Dhoby Ghaut
**Address:** 45 Armenian Street
Singapore 179936 Singapore
**Phone:** +65 6337 7535

#45
**Art Friend**
Art Supplies
**Average price:** Expensive
**District:** Bugis, Bras Brasah
**Address:** 231 Bain Street
Singapore 180231 Singapore
**Phone:** +65 6336 8338

#46
**Orchard Central**
Shopping Center
**Average price:** Expensive
**District:** Somerset, Orchard
**Address:** 181 Orchard Road
Singapore 238896 Singapore
**Phone:** +65 6238 1051

#47
**C K Tang Ltd**
Department Store
**Average price:** Exclusive
**District:** Orchard
**Address:** 310 Orchard Rd
Singapore 238864 Singapore
**Phone:** +65 6737 5500

#48
**SLR Revolution**
Photography Store & Service
**Average price:** Moderate
**District:** City Hall
**Address:** 109 North Bridge Rd
Singapore 179097 Singapore
**Phone:** +65 6336 8767

#49
**Foundry**
Furniture Store
**Average price:** Moderate
**District:** Bras Brasah, City Hall
**Address:** 3 Seah Street
Singapore 188379 Singapore
**Phone:** +65 6339 6381

#50
**A.P.C**
Fashion
**Average price:** Moderate
**District:** Bras Brasah, City Hall
**Address:** Raffles Hotel Arcade,
#02-09, 328 North Bridge Rd
Singapore 188719 Singapore
**Phone:** +65 6224 5501

#51
**Limited Edt Vault**
Shoe Store
**Average price:** Expensive
**District:** Somerset, Orchard
**Address:** 313 Orchard Road,
313 Somerset, 238895 Singapore
**Phone:** +65 6834 4904

#52
**Prada**
Personal Shopping
**Average price:** Exclusive
**District:** Orchard
**Address:** 2 Orchard Turn
Singapore 238801 Singapore
**Phone:** +65 6509 3113

#53
**Early Learning Centre**
Toy Store
**Average price:** Expensive
**District:** Newton, Novena
**Address:** 101 Thomson Road
Singapore 307591 Singapore
**Phone:** +65 6258 0128

#54
**The Cathay**
Shopping Center
**Average price:** Expensive
**District:** Dhoby Ghaut, Orchard
**Address:** 2 Handy Road
Singapore 229233 Singapore
**Phone:** +65 6732 7332

#55
**Bugis Junction**
Shopping Center
**Average price:** Expensive
**District:** Bugis
**Address:** 200 Victoria Street
Singapore 188021 Singapore
**Phone:** +65 6557 6557

#56
**313@Somerset**
Shopping Center
**Average price:** Expensive
**District:** Somerset, Orchard
**Address:** 313 Orchard Rd
Singapore 238895 Singapore
**Phone:** +65 6496 9313

#57
## Nex
Shopping Center
**Average price:** Expensive
**District:** Serangoon
**Address:** 23 Serangoon Central
Singapore 556083 Singapore
**Phone:** +65 6416 6366

#58
## Spotlight
Home Decor
**Average price:** Expensive
**District:** Dhoby Ghaut, Orchard
**Address:** 68 Orchard Rd
Singapore 238839 Singapore
**Phone:** +65 6773 9808

#59
## Ngee Ann City
Shopping Center
**Average price:** Exclusive
**District:** Orchard
**Address:** 391 Orchard Road
Singapore 238872 Singapore
**Phone:** +65 6506 0641

#60
## Paragon
Shopping Center
**Average price:** Exclusive
**District:** Orchard
**Address:** 290 Orchard Road
Singapore 238859 Singapore
**Phone:** +65 6738 5535

#61
## H&M
Men's Clothing, Women's Clothing,
Lingerie
**Average price:** Expensive
**District:** Somerset, Orchard
**Address:** 1 Grange Road
Singapore 239693 Singapore
**Phone:** +65 6235 1459

#62
## Millenia Walk
Shopping Center
**Average price:** Exclusive
**District:** City Hall
**Address:** 9 Raffles Boulevard
Singapore 039596 Singapore
**Phone:** +65 6883 1122

#63
## Bugis Village
Fashion
**Average price:** Expensive
**District:** Bugis
**Address:** 151B Rochor Road
Singapore 188426 Singapore
**Phone:** +65 6338 9513

#64
## Lush
Cosmetics & Beauty Supply
**Average price:** Expensive
**District:** Orchard
**Address:** 435 Orchard Rd
Singapore 238877 Singapore
**Phone:** +65 6732 6758

#65
## Tanglin Mall
Shopping Center
**Average price:** Expensive
**District:** Tanglin
**Address:** 163 Tanglin Road
Singapore 247933 Singapore
**Phone:** +65 6736 4922

#66
## Singapore Island Country Club
Sporting Goods
**Average price:** Expensive
**District:** Ann Siang Hill, Tanjong Pagar
**Address:** 180 Is Club Rd
Singapore 578774 Singapore
**Phone:** +65 6459 2222

#67
## Lomography Gallery
Photography Store & Service
**Average price:** Expensive
**District:** Ann Siang Hill, Tanjong Pagar
**Address:** 295 South Bridge Road
Singapore 058838 Singapore
**Phone:** +65 6223 8850

#68
## Chinatown Complex
Shopping
**Average price:** Moderate
**District:** Chinatown
**Address:** 335 Smith St
Singapore 050335 Singapore
**Phone:** +65 6323 5586

#69
## Parco Next
Department Store
**Average price:** Moderate
**District:** City Hall
**Address:** 9 Raffles Boulevard
Singapore 039596 Singapore
**Phone:** +65 6595 9100

#70
## Charles & Keith
Accessories, Shoe Store
**Average price:** Expensive
**District:** City Hall
**Address:** 1 Raffles Link #B1-32/34
Singapore 039393 Singapore
**Phone:** +65 6338 0913

#71
## Elohim By Sabrinagoh
Women's Clothing
**Average price:** Exclusive
**District:** Dhoby Ghaut, Orchard
**Address:** 181 Orchard Road
Singapore 238896 Singapore
**Phone:** +65 6634 2201

#72
## Tiffany and Co
Jewelry
**Average price:** Expensive
**District:** Orchard
**Address:** 391 Orchard Road
Singapore 238872 Singapore
**Phone:** +65 6735 8823

#73
## River Island
Fashion
**Average price:** Expensive
**District:** Orchard
**Address:** 2 Orchard Turn
Singapore 238801 Singapore
**Phone:** +65 6509 8701

#74
## Hock Siong Waste Dealers
Used, Vintage & Consignment
**Average price:** Expensive
**District:** Macpherson
**Address:** 153 Kampong Ampat
Singapore 368326 Singapore
**Phone:** +65 6281 8338

#75
## Antipodean
Women's Clothing
**Average price:** Exclusive
**District:** Holland Village
**Address:** 27a Lorong Mambong,
Holland Village, 277686 Singapore
**Phone:** +65 6463 7336

#76
## IKEA
Furniture Store
**Average price:** Expensive
**District:** Redhill, Alexandra
**Address:** 317 Alexandra Road
Singapore 159965 Singapore
**Phone:** +65 6786 6868

#77
## Strangelets
Jewelry, Home Decor
**Average price:** Expensive
**District:** Tiong Bahru
**Address:** 7 Yong Siak Street
Singapore 168644 Singapore
**Phone:** +65 6222 1456

#78
## Parkway Parade
Shopping Center
**Average price:** Expensive
**District:** Marine Parade
**Address:** 80 Marine Parade Road
Singapore 449269 Singapore
**Phone:** +65 6344 1242

#85
## Great World City
Shopping Center
**Average price:** Expensive
**District:** River Valley
**Address:** 1 Kim Seng Promenade
Singapore 237994 Singapore
**Phone:** +65 6737 3855

#86
## Arteastiq
Bakeries, Desserts, Coffee & Tea,
Shopping, Cafe
**Average price:** Exclusive
**District:** Somerset, Orchard
**Address:** 333 Orchard Road
Singapore 238867 Singapore
**Phone:** +65 6235 8370

#87
## AMK Hub
Shopping Center
**Average price:** Moderate
**District:** Ang Mo Kio
**Address:** 53 Ang Mo Kio Avenue 3
Singapore 569933 Singapore
**Phone:** +65 6753 9000

#88
## Marina Square
Shopping Center
**Average price:** Expensive
**District:** City Hall
**Address:** 6 Raffles Boulevard
Singapore 039594 Singapore
**Phone:** +65 6339 8787

#89
## Mandarin Gallery
Art Gallery
**Average price:** Moderate
**District:** Somerset, Orchard
**Address:** 333 Orchard Rd
Singapore 238867 Singapore
**Phone:** +65 6737 4411

#90
## Wheelock Place
Shopping Center
**Average price:** Exclusive
**District:** Tanglin
**Address:** 501 Orchard Rd
Singapore 238880 Singapore
**Phone:** +65 6235 7146

#91
**Far East Plaza**
Shopping
**Average price:** Expensive
**District:** Orchard
**Address:** 14 Scotts Rd
Singapore 228213 Singapore
**Phone:** +65 6734 3227

#92
**Holland Village**
Shopping
**Average price:** Moderate
**District:** Holland Village
**Address:** Holland Rd
Singapore 278967 Singapore
**Phone:** +65 6466 7333

#93
**Anchorpoint**
Grocery, Shopping Center, Outlet Store
**Average price:** Expensive
**District:** Queenstown, Alexandra
**Address:** 370 Alexandra Rd
Singapore 159953 Singapore
**Phone:** +65 6475 2257

#94
**I12 Katong**
Shopping Center
**Average price:** Exclusive
**District:** Marine Parade, Katong
**Address:** 112 East Coast Road
Singapore 428802 Singapore
**Phone:** +65 6636 2112

#95
**Challenger**
Computers
**Average price:** Expensive
**District:** City Hall
**Address:** 109 North Bridge Rd,
Funan DigitaLife Mall
Singapore 179097 Singapore
**Phone:** +65 6339 9008

#96
**Tangs VivoCity**
Department Store
**Average price:** Expensive
**District:** Harbourfront
**Address:** 1 Harbourfront Walk
Singapore 098585 Singapore
**Phone:** +65 6737 5500

#97
**Charles & Keith Factory Outlet**
Shoe Store
**Average price:** Expensive
**District:** Queenstown, Alexandra
**Address:** Anchorpoint 370 Alexandra Rd
Singapore 159953 Singapore
**Phone:** +65 6472 6937

#98
**Macshop**
Computers
**Average price:** Expensive
**District:** Clarke Quay
**Address:** 6 Eu Tong Sen Street
Singapore 059817 Singapore
**Phone:** +65 6334 1633

#99
**Popcornpop**
Hobby Shops
**Average price:** Expensive
**District:** Bayfront, City Hall
**Address:** 02-17, Esplanade Mall
Singapore 039802 Singapore
**Phone:** +65 6333 5623

#100
**Singapore Tyler Print Institute**
Art Gallery
**Average price:** Moderate
**District:** Robertson Quay
**Address:** 41 Robertson Quay
Singapore 238236 Singapore
**Phone:** +65 6336 3663

#101
**Topshop & Topman**
Fashion
**Average price:** Expensive
**District:** Bras Brasah, City Hall
**Address:** Raffles City Shopping Centre
252 North Bridge Road
Singapore 179103 Singapore
**Phone:** +65 6339 0117

#102
**Kinokuniya**
Bookstore
**Average price:** Expensive
**District:** Bugis
**Address:** 177 River Valley Road
Singapore 179036 Singapore
**Phone:** +65 6337 1300

#103
**Space**
Furniture Store
**Average price:** Moderate
**District:** Bencoolen
**Address:** 77 Bencoolen Street
Singapore 189653 Singapore
**Phone:** +65 6415 0000

#104
**City Music**
Music & DVDs, Musical Instruments
& Teachers
**Average price:** Expensive
**District:** Mount Sophia
**Address:** 1 Sophia Rd
Singapore 228149 Singapore
**Phone:** +65 6337 7058

#105
**Penhaligon's**
Cosmetics & Beauty Supply
**Average price:** Exclusive
**District:** Orchard
**Address:** 2 Orchard Turn, #03-16
Singapore 238801 Singapore
**Phone:** +65 6634 1040

#106
**Clancy Boutique**
Shopping
**Average price:** Moderate
**District:** Orchard
**Address:** 14 Scotts Rd, #04-89
Singapore 228213 Singapore
**Phone:** +65 6738 6971

#107
**Commune**
Home Decor
**Average price:** Expensive
**District:** City Hall
**Address:** 9 Raffles Boulevard
Singapore 039596 Singapore
**Phone:** +65 6338 3823

#108
**Ruby Photo**
Photography Store & Service
**Average price:** Exclusive
**District:** Bras Brasah
**Address:** 3 Coleman Street
Singapore 179804 Singapore
**Phone:** +65 6338 0236

#109
**Wardah Books**
Bookstore
**Average price:** Expensive
**District:** Arab Street
**Address:** 58 Bussorah St
Singapore 199474 Singapore
**Phone:** +65 6297 1232

#110
**The Reckless Shop**
Women's Clothing
**Average price:** Expensive
**District:** Somerset, Orchard
**Address:** 181 Orchard Road
Singapore 238896 Singapore
**Phone:** +65 6338 8246

#111
**Watsons**
DrugStore, Cosmetics & Beauty Supply
**Average price:** Expensive
**District:** Orchard
**Address:** 391 Orchard Road
Singapore 238872 Singapore
**Phone:** +65 6735 4936

#112
**La Senza**
Fashion
**Average price:** Expensive
**District:** Orchard
**Address:** 290 Orchard Rd
Singapore 238859 Singapore
**Phone:** +65 6333 8611

#113
**Heatwave**
Leather Goods, Shoe Store,
Accessories
**Average price:** Expensive
**District:** Orchard
**Address:** 435 Orchard Rd
Singapore 238877 Singapore
**Phone:** +65 6235 3400

#114
**Toys 'R' Us**
Toy Store
**Average price:** Moderate
**District:** Harbourfront
**Address:** 1 Harbourfront Walk
Singapore 098585 Singapore
**Phone:** +65 6273 0661

#115
**The Birth Shop**
Baby Gear & Furniture
**Average price:** Expensive
**District:** Thomson
**Address:** 22 Sin Ming Lane
Singapore 573969 Singapore
**Phone:** +65 6570 4681

#116
**Lemon Zest**
Kitchen & Bath
**Average price:** Moderate
**District:** Holland Village
**Address:** 43 Jln Merah Saga
Singapore 278115 Singapore
**Phone:** +65 6471 0566

#117
**Gamewerks**
Computers
**Average price:** Expensive
**District:** Clementi, West Coast
**Address:** 442 Clementi Ave 3
Singapore 120442 Singapore
**Phone:** +65 6468 7855

#118
**Mee Mee Optics &
Contact Lens Centre**
Eyewear & Opticians
**Average price:** Moderate
**District:** Bukit Timah, Upper Bukit Timah
**Address:** 1 Jln Anak Bukit
Singapore 588996 Singapore
**Phone:** +65 6466 1028

#119
**Sealy Sleep Boutique**
Mattresses
**Average price:** Exclusive
**District:** Siglap
**Address:** 25 Upper East Coast Rd
Singapore 455290 Singapore
**Phone:** +65 6243 1880

#120
**Big Bookshop**
Bookstore
**Average price:** Moderate
**District:** Tampines
**Address:** Blk 823 Tampines St 81
Singapore 520823 Singapore
**Phone:** +65 6785 1163

#121
**Pluck**
Fashion
**Average price:** Expensive
**District:** Arab Street
**Address:** 31/33 Haji Lane
Singapore 189226 Singapore
**Phone:** +65 6396 4048

#122
**The Tintin Shop**
Hobby Shops
**Average price:** Exclusive
**District:** Chinatown
**Address:** 56 Pagoda St
Singapore 059215 Singapore
**Phone:** +65 8183 2210

#123
**Velocity Novena**
Shopping Center, Sporting Goods
**Average price:** Expensive
**District:** Novena
**Address:** 238 Thomson Rd
Singapore 307683 Singapore
**Phone:** +65 6358 0700

#124
**Wheeler's Yard**
Cafe, Bikes
**Average price:** Moderate
**District:** Novena
**Address:** 28 Lorong Ampas
Singapore 328781 Singapore
**Phone:** +65 6254 9128

#125
**7Adam**
Art Gallery, Modern European
**Average price:** Exclusive
**District:** Bukit Timah
**Address:** 7 Adam Park
Singapore 289926 Singapore
**Phone:** +65 6467 0777

#126
**myVillage**
Shopping Center
**Average price:** Moderate
**District:** Serangoon Gardens
**Address:** 1 Maju Avenue
Singapore 556679 Singapore
**Phone:** +65 6634 2288

#127
**Tampines Mall**
Cosmetics & Beauty Supply,
Department Store, Shopping Center
**Average price:** Expensive
**District:** Tampines
**Address:** 4 Tampines Central 5
Singapore 529510 Singapore
**Phone:** +65 6788 8370

#128
**Causeway Point**
Shopping Center
**Average price:** Expensive
**District:** Woodlands
**Address:** 1 Woodlands Square
Singapore 738099 Singapore
**Phone:** +65 6894 2237

#129
**Granny's Day Out**
Used, Vintage & Consignment
**Average price:** Moderate
**District:** City Hall
**Address:** Peninsula Shopping Centre
#03-25, 3 Coleman Street
Singapore 179804 Singapore
**Phone:** +65 6336 9774

#130
**CityLink Mall**
Shopping Center
**Average price:** Expensive
**District:** City Hall
**Address:** 1 Raffles Link
Singapore 039393 Singapore
**Phone:** +65 6339 9913

#131
**Adidas**
Sporting Goods
**Average price:** Exclusive
**District:** Dhoby Ghaut, Orchard
**Address:** 2 Handy Road #02-06/07
The Cathay, 229233 Singapore
**Phone:** +65 6887 5632

#132
**Liang Court**
Shopping Center, Arts & Entertainment
**Average price:** Moderate
**District:** Bugis
**Address:** 177 River Valley Rd
Singapore 179030 Singapore
**Phone:** +65 6336 7184

#133
**Dulcetfig**
Women's Clothing, Used,
Vintage & Consignment
**Average price:** Expensive
**District:** Arab Street
**Address:** 41 Haji Lane
Singapore 189234 Singapore
**Phone:** +65 6396 9648

#134
**The Centrepoint**
Shopping Center
**Average price:** Moderate
**District:** Somerset, Orchard
**Address:** 176 Orchard Road
Singapore 238843 Singapore
**Phone:** +65 6733 0888

#135
**28th Février**
Art Gallery
**Average price:** Moderate
**District:** Redhill
**Address:** 5 Jln Kilang
Singapore 159405 Singapore
**Phone:** +65 6366 4642

#136
**Lim's Arts & Living**
Arts & Crafts, Furniture Store
**Average price:** Expensive
**District:** Holland Village
**Address:** Holland Road Shopping
Centre
#02-01, 211 Holland Ave
Singapore 278967 Singapore
**Phone:** +65 6467 1300

#137
**Venus Beauty**
Cosmetics & Beauty Supply
**Average price:** Moderate
**District:** Ang Mo Kio
**Address:** 702 Ang Mo Kio Ave 8
#01-2507, Singapore 560702 Singapore
**Phone:** +65 6459 0491

#138
**Jem**
Shopping Center
**Average price:** Expensive
**District:** Jurong
**Address:** 50 Jurong Gateway Road
Singapore 608549 Singapore
**Phone:** +65 6672 9500

#139
**Giant**
Department Store
**Average price:** Moderate
**District:** Tampines
**Address:** 21 Tampines North Drive 2
Singapore 528765 Singapore
**Phone:** +65 6788 5919

#140
**Downtown East**
Shopping Center
**Average price:** Exclusive
**District:** Pasir Ris
**Address:** 1 Pasir Ris Close
Singapore 519599 Singapore
**Phone:** +65 6589 1865

#141
**City Square Mall**
Shopping Center
**Average price:** Expensive
**District:** Little India
**Address:** 180 Kitchener Road
Singapore 208539 Singapore
**Phone:** +65 6595 6595

#142
**Valu$**
Shopping
**Average price:** Moderate
**District:** Boon Lay
**Address:** 1 Jurong West Central 2
Singapore 648886 Singapore
**Phone:** +65 6316 9461

#143
**Challenger**
Electronics, Computers
**Average price:** Expensive
**District:** Boon Lay
**Address:** 1 Jurong West Central 2
Singapore 648886 Singapore
**Phone:** +65 6793 7122

#144
**Chevron House**
Shopping Center
**Average price:** Moderate
**District:** Bayfront, Raffles Place
**Address:** 30 Raffles Place
Singapore 048619 Singapore
**Phone:** +65 6276 0364

#145
**Red Dot Design Museum Shop**
Cards & Stationery
**Average price:** Moderate
**District:** Tanjong Pagar
**Address:** 28 Maxwell Road
Singapore 069120 Singapore
**Phone:** +65 6225 5950

#146
**MUJI**
Shopping
**Average price:** Moderate
**District:** Bayfront
**Address:** 6 Raffles Boulevard
Singapore 039594 Singapore
**Phone:** +65 6336 6123

#147
## Shanghai Tang
Women's Clothing
**Average price:** Exclusive
**District:** Bayfront
**Address:** 10 Bayfront Avenue
Singapore 018956 Singapore
**Phone:** +65 6688 7180

#148
## Hup Leong Co.
Bikes, Bike Repair/Maintenance
**Average price:** Exclusive
**District:** Outram
**Address:** 51 Chin Swee Rd
Singapore 160051 Singapore
**Phone:** +65 6532 3700

#149
## Prints
Cards & Stationery
**Average price:** Exclusive
**District:** City Hall
**Address:** City Link Mall
Singapore 039393 Singapore
**Phone:** +65 6336 3316

#150
## Massimo Dutti
Fashion
**Average price:** Exclusive
**District:** City Hall
**Address:** 6 Raffles Blvd
Singapore 039594 Singapore
**Phone:** +65 6337 6088

#151
## Dorothy Perkins
Women's Clothing, Accessories
**Average price:** Exclusive
**District:** City Hall
**Address:** 6 Raffles Boulevard
Singapore 039594 Singapore
**Phone:** +65 6336 4408

#152
## BonGoût
Shopping
**Average price:** Moderate
**District:** Robertson Quay
**Address:** 60 Robertson Quay
Singapore 238252 Singapore
**Phone:**

#153
## Book Point
Bookstore
**Average price:** Moderate
**District:** Bras Brasah
**Address:** 231 Bain Street, #03-17
Singapore 180231 Singapore
**Phone:** +65 6338 9106

#154
## Flea & Trees
Department Store, Women's Clothing
**Average price:** Expensive
**District:** Tiong Bahru
**Address:** 68 Seng Poh Ln
Singapore 160068 Singapore
**Phone:** +65 8139 1133

#155
## NBC
Office Equipment, Art Supplies,
Cards & Stationery
**Average price:** Moderate
**District:** Bugis
**Address:** 200 Victoria Street
Singapore 188021 Singapore
**Phone:** +65 6339 0793

#156
## The Atrium at Orchard
Shopping Center
**Average price:** Moderate
**District:** Dhoby Ghaut, Orchard
**Address:** 60A/60B Orchard Road
Singapore 238890 Singapore
**Phone:** +65 6332 9770

#157
## TotallyHotStuff
Shopping
**Average price:** Expensive
**District:** Bugis
**Address:** 201 Victoria Street
Singapore 188067 Singapore
**Phone:** +65 6341 9223

#158
## Muji
Shopping
**Average price:** Moderate
**District:** Bugis
**Address:** 230 Victoria Street Bugis
Junction, 188024 Singapore
**Phone:** +65 6273 8833

#159
## Sin Hin Chuan Kee
Arts & Crafts
**Average price:** Moderate
**District:** Arab Street
**Address:** 798 North Bridge Rd
Singapore 198766 Singapore
**Phone:** +65 6298 8000

#160
## The hansel Shop
Fashion
**Average price:** Exclusive
**District:** Somerset, Orchard
**Address:** 333A Orchard Road
Singapore 238867 Singapore
**Phone:** +65 6337 0992

#161
## Hung Brothers
Electronics
**Average price:** Expensive
**District:** Little India
**Address:** 1 Rochor Canal Road
Singapore 188504 Singapore
**Phone:** +65 6336 9989

#162
## M.A.D - Museum of Art & Design
Art Gallery
**Average price:** Expensive
**District:** Somerset, Orchard
**Address:** 333A Orchard Road
Singapore 238897 Singapore
**Phone:** +65 6734 5688

#163
## Simply Flowers
Florists
**Average price:** Moderate
**District:** Orchard
**Address:** 2 Orchard Turn
Singapore 238801 Singapore
**Phone:** +65 6100 1779

#164
## W.E. Workshop Element
Fashion
**Average price:** Exclusive
**District:** Orchard
**Address:** 435 Orchard Road
Singapore 238877 Singapore
**Phone:** +65 6733 3849

#165
## The Body Shop
Cosmetics & Beauty Supply
**Average price:** Expensive
**District:** Orchard
**Address:** 2 Orchard Turn #B2-39
Singapore 238801 Singapore
**Phone:** +65 6513 4505

#166
## EpiCentre
Electronics
**Average price:** Exclusive
**District:** Tanglin
**Address:** 501 Orchard Rd
Singapore 238880 Singapore
**Phone:** +65 6238 9378

#167
## Suit Select
Women's Clothing, Men's Clothing
**Average price:** Moderate
**District:** Tanglin
**Address:** 9 Scotts Road
Singapore 228210 Singapore
**Phone:** +65 6732 1162

#168
## Veronica's Florist Gifts
Florists
**Average price:** Exclusive
**District:** Tanglin
**Address:** 163 Tanglin Rd
Singapore 247933 Singapore
**Phone:** +65 6737 2811

#169
## Skinfood
Skin Care, Cosmetics & Beauty Supply
**Average price:** Expensive
**District:** Novena
**Address:** 10 Sinaran Drive
Singapore 307506 Singapore
**Phone:** +65 6397 6310

#170
## Harvey Norman
Electronics, Computers
**Average price:** Expensive
**District:** Novena
**Address:** 10 Sinaran Drive
Singapore 307506 Singapore
**Phone:** +65 6397 6190

#171
## Swee Lee
Musical Instruments & Teachers
**Average price:** Moderate
**District:** Boon Keng, Geylang
**Address:** 150 Sims Dr #02-00
Singapore 387381 Singapore
**Phone:** +65 6846 3610

#172
## Pedro
Shoe Store
**Average price:** Moderate
**District:** Queenstown, Alexandra
**Address:** 370 Alexandra Road
Singapore 159953 Singapore
**Phone:** +65 6472 6963

#173
## Far East Flora
Florists
**Average price:** Moderate
**District:** Queenstown
**Address:** 590 Queensway
Singapore 149072 Singapore
**Phone:** +65 6472 5365

#174
## Allscript Magazines
Newspapers & Magazines
**Average price:** Moderate
**District:** Marine Parade, Katong
**Address:** 112 E Coast Road
Singapore 428802 Singapore
**Phone:** +65 6636 3870

#175
**Parisilk Electronics & Computers**
Appliances, Electronics,
IT Service & Computer Repair
**Average price:** Expensive
**District:** Holland Village
**Address:** 15A Lorong Liput
Singapore 277730 Singapore
**Phone:** +65 6466 6002

#176
**The Little Happyshop**
Arts & Crafts
**Average price:** Moderate
**District:** Holland Village
**Address:** 3 Lorong Liput
Singapore 277725 Singapore
**Phone:** +65 6466 8995

#177
**My Bike Shop**
Bikes
**Average price:** Exclusive
**District:** West Coast
**Address:** 25 Jln Mas Puteh
Singapore 128630 Singapore
**Phone:** +65 6775 7133

#178
**Kai Bridal Couture**
Bridal
**Average price:** Moderate
**District:** Raffles Place
**Address:** 120a Telok Ayer Street
Singapore 068589 Singapore
**Phone:** +65 6533 2383

#179
**Willow & Huxley**
Fashion
**Average price:** Moderate
**District:** Raffles Place
**Address:** 20 Amoy Street
Singapore 069855 Singapore
**Phone:** +65 6220 1745

#180
**The Arcade**
Shopping Center
**Average price:** Moderate
**District:** Bayfront, Raffles Place
**Address:** 11 Collyer Quay
Singapore 049317 Singapore
**Phone:** +65 6220 9335

#181
**Gentlemen Quarters**
Men's Clothing
**Average price:** Moderate
**District:** Raffles Place
**Address:** 5 Raffles Place #B1-06
Singapore 048618 Singapore
**Phone:** +65 6532 5526

#182
**Ana Boutique**
Women's Clothing
**Average price:** Moderate
**District:** Ann Siang Hill, Tanjong Pagar
**Address:** 86 Club Street
Singapore 069454 Singapore
**Phone:** +65 6221 2897

#183
**Medic Drugstore**
DrugStore
**Average price:** Moderate
**District:** Tanjong Pagar
**Address:** 1 Tanjong Pagar Plaza
Singapore 082001 Singapore
**Phone:** +65 6224 4842

#184
**Swanston**
Cosmetics & Beauty Supply
**Average price:** Moderate
**District:** Outram
**Address:** 101 Upper Cross Street
Singapore 058357 Singapore
**Phone:** +65 6535 6763

#185
**Surrealist Love Scene**
Fashion
**Average price:** Exclusive
**District:** Clarke Quay
**Address:** 22 Sin Ming Lane
Singapore 573969 Singapore
**Phone:** +65 6684 9130

#186
**South Asia Computer**
Computers
**Average price:** Expensive
**District:** City Hall
**Address:** 109 North Bridge Rd
Singapore 179097 Singapore
**Phone:** +65 6337 0871

#187
**Trixilini**
Women's Clothing
**Average price:** Moderate
**District:** City Hall
**Address:** 9 Raffles Boulevard
Singapore 039596 Singapore
**Phone:** +65 6338 7060

#188
**Goodgoods @ Millenia Walk**
Shoe Store, Leather Goods, Accessories
**Average price:** Moderate
**District:** City Hall
**Address:** 9 Raffles Boulevard
Singapore 039596 Singapore
**Phone:** +65 9750 4920

#189
**The Naturally Better Co**
Cosmetics & Beauty Supply
**Average price:** Moderate
**District:** City Hall
**Address:** 9 Raffles Boulevard,
#02-46 Millenia Walk
Singapore 039596 Singapore
**Phone:** +65 6471 7220

#190
**DC Superheroes**
Men's Clothing, Women's Clothing
**Average price:** Moderate
**District:** City Hall
**Address:** Temasek Boulevard 3,
#02-068 Suntec City
Singapore 038983 Singapore
**Phone:** +65 6337 7502

#191
**Vine Vera**
Cosmetics & Beauty Supply
**Average price:** Moderate
**District:** City Hall
**Address:** 3 Temasek Blvd
Singapore 038983 Singapore
**Phone:** +65 6222 5962

#192
**Ebenex Music**
Music & DVDs
**Average price:** Moderate
**District:** City Hall
**Address:** 231 Bain Street
Singapore 180231 Singapore
**Phone:** +65 6345 0253

#193
**Divine Couture**
Bridal
**Average price:** Moderate
**District:** Dhoby Ghaut
**Address:** 5 Tank Road
Singapore 238061 Singapore
**Phone:** +65 6235 7951

#194
**Le Mercier's Fine Furnishings**
Furniture Store, Interior Design,
Lighting Fixtures & Equipment
**Average price:** Exclusive
**District:** Robertson Quay
**Address:** 65 Mohamed Sultan Rd
Singapore 239003 Singapore
**Phone:** +65 6734 3425

#195
**Seng Yew Book Store**
Bookstore
**Average price:** Moderate
**District:** Bugis, Bras Brasah
**Address:** 231 Bain Street
Singapore 180231 Singapore
**Phone:** +65 6336 2447

#196
**Kwong Shin Eyewear**
Eyewear & Opticians
**Average price:** Moderate
**District:** Bugis, Bras Brasah
**Address:** 231 Bain St
Singapore 180231 Singapore
**Phone:** +65 6338 6766

#197
**SKS Books Warehouse**
Bookstore
**Average price:** Moderate
**District:** Tiong Bahru
**Address:** 315 Outram Rd
Singapore 169074 Singapore
**Phone:** +65 6227 9700

#198
**Niños Felices**
Men's Clothing
**Average price:** Moderate
**District:** Arab Street
**Address:** 45 Haji Lane
Singapore 189238 Singapore
**Phone:** +65 6235 5531

#199
**Doinky Doodles**
Fabric Store, Accessories
**Average price:** Moderate
**District:** Arab Street
**Address:** 33 Bali Lane
Singapore 189869 Singapore
**Phone:** +65 6292 2248

#200
**LiveStudios**
Bridal, Photography Store & Service
**Average price:** Moderate
**District:** Mount Sophia
**Address:** 52 Niven Rd
Singapore 228400 Singapore
**Phone:** +65 6250 0791

# TOP 500 RESTAURANTS

Recommended by Locals & Trevelers

(From #1 to #500)

#1
## Restaurant Andre
**Cuisines:** French
**Average price:** Above $61
**District:** Chinatown
**Address:** 41 Bukit Pasoh Road
Singapore 089855 Singapore
**Phone:** +65 6534 8880

#2
## Din Tai Fung
**Cuisines:** Shanghainese,
Taiwanese, Dim Sum
**Average price:** $11-30
**District:** Bayfront
**Address:** 435 Orchard Road
Singapore 238877 Singapore
**Phone:** +65 6732 1383

#3
## Komala Vilas
**Cuisines:** Indian, Vegetarian
**Average price:** Under $10
**District:** Little India
**Address:** 76-78 Serangoon Rd
Singapore 217981 Singapore
**Phone:** +65 6293 6980

#4
## Tian Tian Hainanese Chicken Rice
**Cuisines:** Chinese
**Average price:** Under $10
**District:** Tanjong Pagar
**Address:** 1 Kadayanallur Street
Singapore 069184 Singapore
**Phone:** +65 9691 4852

#5
## Aoki
**Cuisines:** Japanese, Sushi Bar
**Average price:** Above $61
**District:** Tanglin
**Address:** 1 Scotts Rd, #02-14
Singapore 228208 Singapore
**Phone:** +65 6333 8015

#6
## Din Tai Fung
**Cuisines:** Dim Sum, Shanghainese,
Taiwanese
**Average price:** $11-30
**District:** Bayfront
**Address:** 8a Marina Boulevard
Singapore 018981 Singapore
**Phone:** +65 6634 7877

#7
## Blu Kouzina
**Cuisines:** Greek
**Average price:** $31-60
**District:** Bukit Timah
**Address:** 893 Bukit Timah Road
Singapore 589615 Singapore
**Phone:** +65 6875 0872

#8
## Santouka
**Cuisines:** Japanese
**Average price:** $11-30
**District:** Clarke Quay
**Address:** 6 Eu Tong Sen Street
Singapore 059817 Singapore
**Phone:** +65 6224 0668

#9
## Paradise Dynasty
**Cuisines:** Chinese
**Average price:** $31-60
**District:** Orchard
**Address:** 2 Orchard Turn
Singapore 238801 Singapore
**Phone:** +65 6509 9118

#10
## CUT by Wolfgang Puck
**Cuisines:** American, Steakhouses
**Average price:** Above $61
**District:** Bayfront
**Address:** 2 Bayfront Ave # B1-71
Singapore 018972 Singapore
**Phone:** +65 6688 8517

#11
## Jumbo Seafood
**Cuisines:** Seafood
**Average price:** $31-60
**District:** Marine Parade
**Address:** 1206 East Coast Parkway
Singapore 449883 Singapore
**Phone:** +65 6442 3435

#12
## Ippudo
**Cuisines:** Japanese
**Average price:** $11-30
**District:** Somerset, Orchard
**Address:** 333A Orchard Road
Singapore 238897 Singapore
**Phone:** +65 6235 2797

#13
## Shinji By Kanesaka
**Cuisines:** Japanese, Sushi Bar
**Average price:** Above $61
**District:** Bras Brasah, City Hall
**Address:** 1 Beach Road
Singapore 189673 Singapore
**Phone:** +65 6338 6131

#14
## Saveur
**Cuisines:** French
**Average price:** $11-30
**District:** Bugis, Bras Brasah, City Hall
**Address:** 5 Purvis St
Singapore 188584 Singapore
**Phone:** +65 6333 3121

#15
## Flor Patisserie
**Cuisines:** Japanese, Bakeries
**Average price:** $11-30
**District:** Duxton Hill, Tanjong Pagar
**Address:** 2 Duxton Hill
Singapore 089588 Singapore
**Phone:** +65 6223 8628

#16
## Song Fa Bak Kut Teh
**Cuisines:** Chinese
**Average price:** Under $10
**District:** Clarke Quay
**Address:** 11 New Bridge Road
Singapore 059383 Singapore
**Phone:** +65 6533 6128

#17
## Maison Ikkoku
**Cuisines:** Cafe, Coffee & Tea,
Cocktail Bar
**Average price:** $11-30
**District:** Arab Street
**Address:** 20 Kandahar Street
Singapore 198885 Singapore
**Phone:** +65 6294 0078

#18
## Artichoke Cafe & Bar
**Cuisines:** Bars, Cafe
**Average price:** $11-30
**District:** Bencoolen
**Address:** 161 Middle Rd
Singapore 188977 Singapore
**Phone:** +65 6336 6949

#19
## Restaurant Ember
**Cuisines:** Modern European
**Average price:** $31-60
**District:** Chinatown
**Address:** 50 Keong Saik Road
Singapore 089154 Singapore
**Phone:** +65 6347 1928

#20
## Ristorante da Valentino
**Cuisines:** Italian
**Average price:** $31-60
**District:** Bukit Timah
**Address:** 200 Turf Club Road
Singapore 287994 Singapore
**Phone:** +65 6462 0555

#21
## Burnt Ends
**Cuisines:** Australian
**Average price:** Above $61
**District:** Chinatown
**Address:** 20 Teck Lim Road
Singapore 088391 Singapore
**Phone:** +65 6224 3933

#22
## Catalunya
**Cuisines:** Spanish, Tapas
**Average price:** Above $61
**District:** Bayfront, Raffles Place
**Address:** 82 Collyer Quay
Singapore 049327 Singapore
**Phone:** +65 6534 0886

#23
## Ramen Keisuke Tori King
**Cuisines:** Japanese
**Average price:** $11-30
**District:** Tanjong Pagar
**Address:** 100AM 100 Tras Street
Singapore 079027 Singapore
**Phone:** +65 6604 6861

#24
## Kazu Sumiyaki
**Cuisines:** Japanese
**Average price:** $11-30
**District:** Somerset, Orchard
**Address:** 5 Koek Rd
Singapore 228796 Singapore
**Phone:** +65 6734 2492

#25
## Hainanese Delicacy
## Chicken Rice
**Cuisines:** Chinese
**Average price:** Under $10
**District:** Orchard
**Address:** 14 Scotts Road Far East Plaza
Singapore 228213 Singapore
**Phone:** +65 6734 0639

#26
## Din Tai Fung
**Cuisines:** Taiwanese
**Average price:** $11-30
**District:** Bayfront
**Address:** 2 Bayfront Avenue
Singapore 018972 Singapore
**Phone:** +65 6634 9969

#27
## Din Tai Fung
**Cuisines:** Chinese
**Average price:** $11-30
**District:** Bras Brasah, City Hall
**Address:** 252 North Bridge Road
Singapore 179103 Singapore
**Phone:** +65 6336 6369

#28
## Pizzeria Mozza
**Cuisines:** Italian, Pizza
**Average price:** $31-60
**District:** Bayfront
**Address:** 10 Bayfront Avenue, #B1-42-
46 Singapore 018956 Singapore
**Phone:** +65 6688 8522

#29
**Mezza9**
**Cuisines:** Asian Fusion
**Average price:** $31-60
**District:** Orchard
**Address:** 10 Scotts Road
Singapore 228211 Singapore
**Phone:** +65 6732 1234

#30
**Mellben Seafood**
**Cuisines:** Seafood
**Average price:** $11-30
**District:** Ang Mo Kio
**Address:** 232 Ang Mo Kio Avenue 3
Singapore 560232 Singapore
**Phone:** +65 6285 6762

#31
**Zam Zam**
**Cuisines:** Indian
**Average price:** Under $10
**District:** Arab Street
**Address:** 699 North Bridge Rd
Singapore 198676 Singapore
**Phone:** +65 6298 7011

#32
**StraitsKitchen**
**Cuisines:** Chinese, Indian
**Average price:** $31-60
**District:** Orchard
**Address:** 10 Scotts Road,Lobby Level
Singapore 228211 Singapore
**Phone:** +65 6738 1234

#33
**Arnold's Fried Chicken**
**Cuisines:** Fast Food
**Average price:** Under $10
**District:** Tanjong Rhu, Geylang
**Address:** 810 Geylang Road
Singapore 409286 Singapore
**Phone:** +65 6746 2372

#34
**Hill Street Tai Hwa Pork Noodle**
**Cuisines:** Chinese, Local Flavor
**Average price:** Under $10
**District:** Lavender
**Address:** 466 Crawford Lane
Singapore 190465 Singapore
**Phone:** +65 6292 7477

#35
**Keisuke Tonkotsu King**
**Cuisines:** Japanese
**Average price:** $11-30
**District:** Tanjong Pagar
**Address:** 1 Tras Link
Singapore 078867 Singapore
**Phone:** +65 6636 0855

#36
**Annalakshmi**
**Cuisines:** Indian, Vegetarian
**Average price:** Under $10
**District:** Clarke Quay
**Address:** 20 Havelock Road
Singapore 059765 Singapore
**Phone:** +65 6339 9993

#37
**Itacho Sushi**
**Cuisines:** Japanese, Sushi Bar
**Average price:** $11-30
**District:** Orchard
**Address:** 2 Orchard Turn, #B2-18
Singapore 238801 Singapore
**Phone:** +65 6509 8911

#38
**Hai Di Lao Hot Pot**
**Cuisines:** Chinese
**Average price:** $31-60
**District:** Clarke Quay
**Address:** 3D River Valley Road, #02-04
Singapore 179023 Singapore
**Phone:** +65 6337 8626

#39
**Latteria Mozzarella Bar**
**Cuisines:** Italian
**Average price:** $31-60
**District:** Duxton Hill, Tanjong Pagar
**Address:** 40 Duxton Hill
Singapore 089618 Singapore
**Phone:** +65 6866 1988

#40
**328 Katong Laksa**
**Cuisines:** Fast Food
**Average price:** Under $10
**District:** Marine Parade, Katong
**Address:** 51 East Coast Road
Singapore 428770 Singapore
**Phone:** +65 9732 8163

#41
**Buko Nero**
**Cuisines:** Italian
**Average price:** Above $61
**District:** Duxton Hill, Tanjong Pagar
**Address:** 126 Tanjong Pagar Rd
Singapore 088534 Singapore
**Phone:** +65 6324 6225

#42
**The Soup Spoon UNION**
**Cuisines:** Salad, Soup, Sandwiches
**Average price:** Under $10
**District:** Bras Brasah, City Hall
**Address:** 252 North Bridge Road
Singapore 179103 Singapore
**Phone:** +65 6334 3220

#43
**Going Om**
**Cuisines:** Bars, Cafe
**Average price:** $11-30
**District:** Arab Street
**Address:** 63 Haji Lane
Singapore 189256 Singapore
**Phone:** +65 6297 9197

#44
**Nantsuttei**
**Cuisines:** Japanese
**Average price:** Under $10
**District:** City Hall
**Address:** 9 Raffles Boulevard, #03-02
Singapore 039596 Singapore
**Phone:** +65 6337 7166

#45
**No Signboard Seafood
Restaurant**
**Cuisines:** Seafood
**Average price:** $31-60
**District:** Geylang
**Address:** Geylang 414
Singapore 389392 Singapore
**Phone:** +65 6842 3415

#46
**PS.Cafe**
**Cuisines:** Modern European, Cafe
**Average price:** $11-30
**District:** Queenstown, Dempsey Hill
**Address:** 28B Harding Road
Singapore 249549 Singapore
**Phone:** +65 6479 3343

#47
**Gunther's**
**Cuisines:** French
**Average price:** $11-30
**District:** Bugis, Bras Brasah, City Hall
**Address:** 36 Purvis St
Singapore 188613 Singapore
**Phone:** +65 6338 8955

#48
**Tsukada Nojo**
**Cuisines:** Japanese
**Average price:** $31-60
**District:** Dhoby Ghaut, Orchard
**Address:** 68 Orchard Road, #03-81
Singapore 238891 Singapore
**Phone:** +65 6336 5003

#49
**Department of Caffeine**
**Cuisines:** Cafe
**Average price:** $11-30
**District:** Duxton Hill, Tanjong Pagar
**Address:** 15 Duxton Road
Singapore 089481 Singapore
**Phone:** +65 6223 3426

#50
**Ah Loy Thai**
**Cuisines:** Thai
**Average price:** $11-30
**District:** Bugis
**Address:** 100 Beach Road
Singapore 189702 Singapore
**Phone:** +65 9165 1543

#51
**Holland Village XO Fish Head
Bee Hun Restaurant**
**Cuisines:** Chinese
**Average price:** $11-30
**District:** Dover
**Address:** 19A Dover Crescent
Singapore 131019 Singapore
**Phone:** +65 6778 3691

#52
**Togi Korean**
**Cuisines:** Korean
**Average price:** $11-30
**District:** Chinatown
**Address:** 11 Mosque St
Singapore 059491 Singapore
**Phone:** +65 6221 0830

#53
**Carpenter and Cook**
**Cuisines:** Bakeries, Cafe, Home Decor
**Average price:** $11-30
**District:** Upper Bukit Timah
**Address:** 19 Lorong Kilat
Singapore 598120 Singapore
**Phone:** +65 6463 3648

#54
**Chye Seng Huat Hardware**
**Cuisines:** Cafe, Coffee & Tea
**Average price:** Under $10
**District:** Little India
**Address:** 150 Tyrwhitt Road
Singapore 207563 Singapore
**Phone:** +65 6396 0609

#55
**Ippudo x Tao**
**Cuisines:** Food, Japanese, Bar
**Average price:** $11-30
**District:** Robertson Quay
**Address:** 207 River Valley Road
Singapore 238275 Singapore
**Phone:** +65 6887 5315

#56
**Swee Choon Tim Sum**
**Cuisines:** Dim Sum
**Average price:** Under $10
**District:** Little India
**Address:** 191 Jln Besar
Singapore 208882 Singapore
**Phone:** +65 6294 5292

#57
**Riders Cafe**
**Cuisines:** Breakfast & Brunch
**Average price:** $11-30
**District:** Bukit Timah
**Address:** 51 Fairways Drive
Singapore 286965 Singapore
**Phone:** +65 6466 9819

#58
**DB Bistro Moderne**
**Cuisines:** Modern European
**Average price:** Above $61
**District:** Bayfront
**Address:** 2 Bayfront Avenue
Singapore 018972 Singapore
**Phone:** +65 6688 8525

#59
**The Banana Leaf Apollo**
**Cuisines:** Health Markets, Indian
**Average price:** $11-30
**District:** Little India
**Address:** 48 Serangoon Road
Singapore 217959 Singapore
**Phone:** +65 6298 9184

#60
**Le Bistrot Du Sommelier**
**Cuisines:** French
**Average price:** Above $61
**District:** Bras Brasah, Dhoby Ghaut
**Address:** 53 Armenian Street
Singapore 179940 Singapore
**Phone:** +65 6333 1982

#61
**Tonkatsu Ma Maison**
**Cuisines:** Japanese
**Average price:** $31-60
**District:** Somerset, Orchard
**Address:** 333A Orchard Road
Singapore 238897 Singapore
**Phone:** +65 6733 4541

#62
**Liberty Coffee**
**Cuisines:** Coffee & Tea, Cafe
**Average price:** Under $10
**District:** Farrer Park
**Address:** 131 Rangoon Rd
Singapore 218409 Singapore
**Phone:** +65 6392 2903

#63
**Imperial Treasure Super Peking Duck**
**Cuisines:** Chinese
**Average price:** Above $61
**District:** Orchard
**Address:** 290 Orchard Road
Singapore 238859 Singapore
**Phone:** +65 6732 7838

#64
**Toast Box**
**Cuisines:**
**Average price:** Under $10
**District:** Little India
**Address:** 180 Kitchener Road
Singapore 208539 Singapore
**Phone:** +65 6509 8340

#65
**Taste Paradise**
**Cuisines:** Dim Sum
**Average price:** $11-30
**District:** Orchard
**Address:** 2 Orchard Turn
Singapore 238801 Singapore
**Phone:** +65 6238 8228

#66
**Luke's Oyster Bar & Chop House**
**Cuisines:** Seafood, American
**Average price:** Above $61
**District:** Raffles Place
**Address:** 20 Gemmill Lane
Singapore 069256 Singapore
**Phone:** +65 6221 4468

#67
**The Blue Ginger**
**Cuisines:** Chinese
**Average price:** $31-60
**District:** Tanjong Pagar
**Address:** 97 Tanjong Pagar Road
Singapore 088518 Singapore
**Phone:** +65 6222 3928

#68
**The Plain**
**Cuisines:** Cafe
**Average price:** Under $10
**District:** Tanjong Pagar
**Address:** 50 Craig Rd
Singapore 089688 Singapore
**Phone:** +65 6225 4387

#69
**Flock Café**
**Cuisines:** Cafe
**Average price:** $11-30
**District:** Tiong Bahru
**Address:** 78 Moh Guan Terrace
Singapore 162078 Singapore
**Phone:** +65 6536 3938

#70
**Cicheti**
**Cuisines:** Wine Bars, Italian, Pizza
**Average price:** $11-30
**District:** Arab Street
**Address:** 52 Kandahar Street
Singapore 198901 Singapore
**Phone:** +65 6292 5012

#71
## Salt Tapas & Bar
## by Luke Mangan
**Cuisines:** Spanish, European, Tapas
**Average price:** Above $61
**District:** Bras Brasah, City Hall
**Address:** 252 North Bridge Road,
Raffles City Shopping Centre
Singapore 179103 Singapore
**Phone:** +65 6837 0995

#72
## Eco Gourmet Cafe
**Cuisines:** Asian Fusion
**Average price:** $11-30
**District:** Labrador Park
**Address:** 30 Labrador Villa Road
Singapore 119189 Singapore
**Phone:** +65 6479 8885

#73
## Etna
**Cuisines:** Italian, Vegetarian, Pizza
**Average price:** $11-30
**District:** Duxton Hill, Tanjong Pagar
**Address:** 49/50 Duxton Road
Singapore 089514 Singapore
**Phone:** +65 6220 5513

#74
## Bosses Restaurant
**Cuisines:** Asian Fusion, Dim Sum
**Average price:** $11-30
**District:** Harbourfront
**Address:** 1 Harbourfront Walk
Singapore 098585 Singapore
**Phone:** +65 6376 9740

#75
## Basilico
**Cuisines:** Italian
**Average price:** $31-60
**District:** Tanglin
**Address:** 1 Cuscaden Road
Singapore 249715 Singapore
**Phone:** +65 6725 3232

#76
## Xing Ji Ruo Cuo Mian
**Cuisines:** Chinese
**Average price:** Under $10
**District:** Simei, Bedok North
**Address:** Block 85 Bedok North Street 4
Singapore 460085 Singapore
**Phone:** +65 9835 7884

#77
## Toby's Estate
**Cuisines:** Coffee & Tea, Cafe
**Average price:** $11-30
**District:** Robertson Quay
**Address:** 8 Rodyk St
Singapore 238216 Singapore
**Phone:** +65 6636 7629

#78
## Mortons Steak House
**Cuisines:** American, Steakhouses
**Average price:** Above $61
**District:** Lavender
**Address:** 5 Raffles Avenue, Marina
Square
Singapore 039797 Singapore
**Phone:** +65 6339 3740

#79
## Sarnies
**Cuisines:** Cafe
**Average price:** $11-30
**District:** Raffles Place
**Address:** 136 Telok Ayer Street
Singapore 068601 Singapore
**Phone:** +65 6224 6091

#80
## JiBiru Craft Beer Bar
**Cuisines:** Japanese, Bar
**Average price:** $11-30
**District:** Somerset, Orchard
**Address:** 313 Somerset
Singapore 238895 Singapore
**Phone:** +65 6732 6884

#81
## Lagnaa Barefoot Dining
**Cuisines:** Indian, Lounges, Fondue
**Average price:** $31-60
**District:** Little India
**Address:** 6 Upper Dickson Road
Singapore 207466 Singapore
**Phone:** +65 6296 1215

#82
## Violet Oon's Kitchen
**Cuisines:** Cafe, Breakfast & Brunch
**Average price:** $11-30
**District:** Bukit Timah
**Address:** 881 Bukit Timah Road
Singapore 279893 Singapore
**Phone:** +65 6468 5430

#83
## Ivins
**Cuisines:** Chinese
**Average price:** Under $10
**District:** Bukit Timah
**Address:** 21 Binjai Park
Singapore 589827 Singapore
**Phone:** +65 6468 3060

#84
## OverEasy
**Cuisines:** Bars, Diners, American
**Average price:** $11-30
**District:** Bayfront, Raffles Place
**Address:** 1 Fullerton Rd
Singapore 049213 Singapore
**Phone:** +65 6423 0701

#85
## Tim Ho Wan Singapore
**Cuisines:** Dim Sum
**Average price:** $11-30
**District:** Dhoby Ghaut, Orchard
**Address:** 68 Orchard Road
Singapore 238839 Singapore
**Phone:** +65 6251 2000

#86
## Superstar K
**Cuisines:** Korean
**Average price:** $31-60
**District:** Duxton Hill, Tanjong Pagar
**Address:** 75 Tanjong Pagar Road
Singapore 088496 Singapore
**Phone:** +65 6224 0504

#87
## Praelum Wine Bistro
**Cuisines:** Wine Bars, Cafe
**Average price:** $31-60
**District:** Duxton Hill, Tanjong Pagar
**Address:** 4 Duxton Hill
Singapore 089590 Singapore
**Phone:** +65 6238 5287

#88
## Zhong Guo La Mian Xiao Long Bao
**Cuisines:** Shanghainese
**Average price:** Under $10
**District:** Chinatown
**Address:** Blk 335 Smith Street
Singapore 051335 Singapore
**Phone:** +65 9743 5287

#89
## Ruth's Chris Steak House
**Cuisines:** Steakhouses
**Average price:** Above $61
**District:** City Hall
**Address:** 6 Raffles Boulevard, 4th Floor
Singapore 039594 Singapore
**Phone:** +65 6336 9093

#90
## Nanbantei Japanese
**Cuisines:** Japanese
**Average price:** $11-30
**District:** Orchard
**Address:** 14 Scotts Rd
Singapore 228213 Singapore
**Phone:** +65 6733 5666

#91
## Thai Pan Restaurant
**Cuisines:** Thai
**Average price:** $11-30
**District:** Marine Parade
**Address:** 13 Siglap Road
Singapore 448912 Singapore
**Phone:** +65 6448 9827

#92
## New Ubin Seafood
**Cuisines:** Seafood
**Average price:** $11-30
**District:** Thomson
**Address:** Blk 27 Sin Ming
Industrial Estate Sector A #01-174
Singapore 575680 Singapore
**Phone:** +65 6466 9558

#93
## Little Part 1
**Cuisines:** Bars, American
**Average price:** $11-30
**District:** Thomson
**Address:** 15 Jasmine Road
Singapore 576584 Singapore
**Phone:** +65 6451 7553

#94
## Chicken Up
**Cuisines:** Korean, Fast Food, Pubs
**Average price:** $11-30
**District:** Duxton Hill, Tanjong Pagar
**Address:** 48 Tanjong Pagar Road
Singapore 088469 Singapore
**Phone:** +65 6327 1203

#95
## 8 Korean BBQ
**Cuisines:** Korean
**Average price:** $31-60
**District:** Clarke Quay
**Address:** 6 Eu Tong Sen Street,
#02-70/90 Singapore 059817 Singapore
**Phone:** +65 6222 2159

#96
## Orihara Shouten
**Cuisines:** Bars, Japanese
**Average price:** $11-30
**District:** Robertson Quay
**Address:** 11 Unity St
Singapore 237995 Singapore
**Phone:** +65 6836 5710

#97
## Nagae
**Cuisines:** Japanese
**Average price:** $11-30
**District:** River Valley
**Address:** 392 Havelock Road
Singapore 169663 Singapore
**Phone:** +65 6737 1708

#98
## Wild Honey
**Cuisines:** Breakfast & Brunch
**Average price:** $31-60
**District:** Orchard
**Address:** 6 Scotts Road, #03-01
Scotts Square 228209 Singapore
**Phone:** +65 6636 1816

#99
## Dempsey Hill
**Average price:** $11-30
**District:** Queenstown, Dempsey Hill
**Address:** Blk 8D Dempsey Road
Singapore 249679 Singapore
**Phone:** +65 6472 1868

#100
## Suprette
**Cuisines:** Bars, American
**Average price:** $31-60
**District:** Little India
**Address:** 383 Jalan Besar
Singapore 209001 Singapore
**Phone:** +65 6298 8962

#101
## Ma Maison
**Cuisines:** French, Japanese
**Average price:** $31-60
**District:** Clarke Quay
**Address:** 6 Eu Tong Sen Street
Singapore 059817 Singapore
**Phone:** +65 6327 8122

#102
## Culina
**Cuisines:** Bistro
**Average price:** $31-60
**District:** Queenstown, Dempsey Hill
**Address:** 8 Dempsey Road
Singapore 247696 Singapore
**Phone:** +65 6474 7338

#103
## Choupinette
**Cuisines:** Coffee & Tea, Bistro
**Average price:** $11-30
**District:** Bukit Timah
**Address:** 607 Bukit Timah Road
Singapore 269708 Singapore
**Phone:** +65 6466 0613

#104
## Yakiniku Yazawa
**Cuisines:** Japanese
**Average price:** Above $61
**District:** Robertson Quay
**Address:** 11 Unity Street
Singapore 237995 Singapore
**Phone:** +65 6235 2941

#105
## Bob's Bar
**Cuisines:** Desserts, Cafe, Bar
**Average price:** $11-30
**District:** Harbourfront
**Address:** 1 The Knolls
Singapore 098297 Singapore
**Phone:** +65 6591 5047

#106
## Kampong Glam Cafe
**Cuisines:** Indonesian
**Average price:** Under $10
**District:** Arab Street
**Address:** 17 Bussorah Street
Singapore 199438 Singapore
**Phone:** +65 9385 9452

#107
## Salt Grill & Sky Bar
**Cuisines:** European, Australian
**Average price:** Above $61
**District:** Orchard
**Address:** 2 Orchard Turn, Level 55-56
Singapore 238801 Singapore
**Phone:** +65 6592 5118

#108
## Ssikkek Korean Grill BBQ Buffet
**Cuisines:** Korean, Buffets
**Average price:** $11-30
**District:** Newton, Novena
**Address:** 101 Thomson Road
Singapore 307591 Singapore
**Phone:** +65 6254 8123

#109
## Infuzi
**Cuisines:** French
**Average price:** $11-30
**District:** One-North
**Address:** 10 Biopolis Rd, 01-01
Chromos Blk, 138670 Singapore
**Phone:** +65 6478 9091

#110
## Omakase Burger
**Cuisines:** Burgers
**Average price:** $11-30
**District:** Bukit Timah
**Address:** 200 Turf Club Road
Singapore 287994 Singapore
**Phone:** +65 6763 2698

#111
## Loysel's Toy
**Cuisines:** Coffee & Tea, Cafe
**Average price:** $11-30
**District:** Lavender
**Address:** 66 Kampong Bugis
Singapore 338987 Singapore
**Phone:** +65 6292 2306

#112
## The Clan Restaurant
**Cuisines:** Modern European
**Average price:** Above $61
**District:** Chinatown
**Address:** 18/20 Bukit Pasoh Road
Singapore 089832 Singapore
**Phone:** +65 6222 2084

#113
## IKYU
**Cuisines:** Japanese, Sushi Bar
**Average price:** $31-60
**District:** Tiong Bahru
**Address:** 5 Yong Siak Street
Singapore 168643 Singapore
**Phone:** +65 6223 9003

#114
## Yet Con
**Cuisines:** Chinese
**Average price:** Under $10
**District:** Bugis, Bras Brasah, City Hall
**Address:** 25 Purvis Street
Singapore 188602 Singapore
**Phone:** +65 6337 6819

#115
## Brotzeit
**Cuisines:** German
**Average price:** $31-60
**District:** Harbourfront
**Address:** 1 Harbourfront Walk
Singapore 098585 Singapore
**Phone:** +65 6272 8815

#116
## Penny University
**Cuisines:** Coffee & Tea, Cafe
**Average price:** Under $10
**District:** Siglap, Marine Parade
**Address:** 402 East Coast Road
Singapore 428997 Singapore
**Phone:** +65 9008 9314

#117
## Chicken Rice & Roasted Meat Stall Koufu Food Court
**Cuisines:** Asian Fusion, Chinese
**Average price:** Under $10
**District:** Changi
**Address:** #02-313 Loyang Point
Singapore 510258 Singapore
**Phone:** +65 6506 0161

#118
## Windowsill Pies
**Cuisines:** Bakeries, Cafe
**Average price:** Under $10
**District:** Lavender
**Address:** 78 Horne Road
Singapore 209078 Singapore
**Phone:** +65 9004 7827

#119
## Chippy British Take Away
**Cuisines:** Desserts, British, Fish & Chips
**Average price:** Under $10
**District:** Bras Brasah, City Hall
**Address:** 252 North Bridge Road
Singapore 179103 Singapore
**Phone:** +65 6875 3472

#120
## Satsuma Shochu Dining Bar
**Cuisines:** Japanese, Bar
**Average price:** $11-30
**District:** Robertson Quay
**Address:** 1 Nanson Road, #01-10/#02-10 Singapore 238909 Singapore
**Phone:** +65 6235 3565

#121
## Din Tai Fung
**Average price:** $11-30
**District:** Orchard
**Address:** 290 Orchard Road
Singapore 238859 Singapore
**Phone:** +65 6836 8336

#122
## The Sushi Bar
**Cuisines:** Sushi Bars, Japanese
**Average price:** $11-30
**District:** Orchard
**Address:** 14 Scotts Road
Singapore 228213 Singapore
**Phone:** +65 9625 0861

#123
## Raj
**Cuisines:** Indian
**Average price:** $11-30
**District:** One-North
**Address:** 20 Biopolis Way
Singapore 138668 Singapore
**Phone:** +65 6478 9495

#124
## Salad Stop!
**Cuisines:** Salad
**Average price:** Under $10
**District:** One-North
**Address:** No 1, Fusionopolis Way
Singapore 138632 Singapore
**Phone:** +65 6463 2003

#125
## Nam Nam Noodle Bar
**Cuisines:** Vietnamese
**Average price:** Under $10
**District:** Tanglin
**Address:** 501 Orchard Road
Singapore 238880 Singapore
**Phone:** +65 6735 1488

#126
## Chat Masala
**Cuisines:** Indian
**Average price:** $11-30
**District:** Siglap
**Address:** 158 Upper East Coast Rd
Singapore 455254 Singapore
**Phone:** +65 6876 0570

#127
## Café Le Caire
**Cuisines:** Middle Eastern
**Average price:** Under $10
**District:** Arab Street
**Address:** 39 Arab Street
Singapore 199736 Singapore
**Phone:** +65 6292 0979

#128
## The Coastal Settlement
**Cuisines:** Bars, Breakfast & Brunch
**Average price:** $31-60
**District:** Changi
**Address:** 200 Netheravon Road
Singapore 508529 Singapore
**Phone:** +65 6475 0200

#129
## Kilo at PACT
**Cuisines:** Asian Fusion
**Average price:** $11-30
**District:** Somerset, Orchard
**Address:** 181 Orchard Road,
Orchard Central 238896 Singapore
**Phone:** +65 6884 7560

#130
## Chili's
**Cuisines:** American
**Average price:** Under $10
**District:** Tanglin
**Address:** 163 Tanglin Rd
Singapore 247933 Singapore
**Phone:** +65 6733 3317

#131
## Peperoni Pizzeria
**Cuisines:** Italian
**Average price:** $11-30
**District:** Bukit Timah
**Address:** 4 Greenwood Ave
Singapore 289195 Singapore
**Phone:** +65 6465 6556

#132
## Ramen Champion
**Cuisines:** Japanese
**Average price:** $11-30
**District:** Bugis
**Address:** 201 Victoria Street
Singapore 188067 Singapore
**Phone:** +65 6339 1440

#133
## The Naked Finn
**Cuisines:** Seafood, Pubs
**Average price:** Above $61
**District:** Alexandra
**Address:** 41 Malan Road
Singapore 109454 Singapore
**Phone:** +65 6694 0807

#134
## Esquina
**Cuisines:** Spanish
**Average price:** Above $61
**District:** Chinatown
**Address:** 16 Jiak Chuan Rd
Singapore 089267 Singapore
**Phone:** +65 6222 1616

#135
## Standing Sushi Bar
**Cuisines:** Japanese, Bars, Sushi Bar
**Average price:** $11-30
**District:** Bras Brasah
**Address:** 8 Queen Street
Singapore 188535 Singapore
**Phone:** +65 6333 1335

#136
## Menya Musashi
**Cuisines:** Japanese
**Average price:** $11-30
**District:** Bras Brasah, City Hall
**Address:** 252 North Bridge Road
Singapore 179103 Singapore
**Phone:** +65 6336 6500

#137
## Café Iguana
**Cuisines:** Lounges, Tapas, Mexican
**Average price:** $11-30
**District:** Clarke Quay
**Address:** 30 Merchant Rd
Singapore 058282 Singapore
**Phone:** +65 6236 1275

#138
## Uma Uma Ramen
**Cuisines:** Japanese
**Average price:** $11-30
**District:** Tanglin
**Address:** 583 Orchard Road
Singapore 238884 Singapore
**Phone:** +65 6235 0855

#139
## Wimbly Lu Chocolate
**Cuisines:** Cafe
**Average price:** $11-30
**District:** Serangoon
**Address:** 15-2 Jln Riang
Singapore 358987 Singapore
**Phone:** +65 6289 1489

#140
## Chock Full Of Beans
**Cuisines:** Coffee & Tea, Cafe
**Average price:** $11-30
**District:** Changi
**Address:** 4 Changi Village Road
Singapore 500004 Singapore
**Phone:** +65 6214 8839

#141
## IndoChine Waterfront
**Cuisines:** Asian Fusion
**Average price:** $31-60
**District:** City Hall
**Address:** 1 Empress Pl
Singapore 179555 Singapore
**Phone:** +65 6339 1720

#142
## Pasta Brava
**Cuisines:** Italian
**Average price:** $11-30
**District:** Duxton Hill, Tanjong Pagar
**Address:** 11 Craig Road
Singapore 089671 Singapore
**Phone:** +65 6227 7550

#143
## Wild Rocket
**Cuisines:** Asian Fusion
**Average price:** $11-30
**District:** Mount Sophia
**Address:** 10a Upper Wilkie Rd
Singapore 228119 Singapore
**Phone:** +65 6339 9448

#144
## Marché
**Average price:** $11-30
**District:** Harbourfront
**Address:** 1 Harbourfront Walk
Singapore 098585 Singapore
**Phone:** +65 6376 8226

#145
## La Pizzaiola
**Cuisines:** Italian, Pizza
**Average price:** $11-30
**District:** Serangoon
**Address:** 15-3 Jalan Riang
Singapore 358987 Singapore
**Phone:** +65 6282 5031

#146
## Kinki Restaurant & Bar
**Cuisines:** Japanese, Sushi Bar
**Average price:** $31-60
**District:** Bayfront, Raffles Place
**Address:** 70 Collyer Quay
Singapore 049323 Singapore
**Phone:** +65 6533 3471

#147
## Waku Ghin
**Cuisines:** Asian Fusion
**Average price:** $11-30
**District:** Bayfront
**Address:** 10 Bayfront Avenue,
Level 2 Marina Bay Sands
Singapore 018956 Singapore
**Phone:** +65 6888 8507

#148
## Maki-San
**Cuisines:** Japanese
**Average price:** $11-30
**District:** Dhoby Ghaut, Mount Sophia
**Address:** 2 Handy Road
Singapore 229233 Singapore
**Phone:** +65 6737 8772

#149
## Tonkotsu King Four Seasons
**Cuisines:** Japanese
**Average price:** $11-30
**District:** Bugis
**Address:** 158 Rochor Road
Singapore 188433 Singapore
**Phone:** +65 6333 5740

#150
## Riverside Indonesian BBQ
**Cuisines:** Indonesian
**Average price:** Under $10
**District:** Dhoby Ghaut, Mount Sophia
**Address:** 68 Orchard Rd #06-15/20
Singapore 238839 Singapore
**Phone:** +65 6883 1440

#151
## Mang Kiko's Lechon
**Cuisines:** Filipino, Barbeque
**Average price:** Under $10
**District:** Somerset, Orchard
**Address:** 121 Somerset Road
Singapore 238166 Singapore
**Phone:** +65 6646 6444

#152
## Long Beach King Seafood
**Cuisines:** Seafood
**Average price:** Above $61
**District:** Kallang, Mountbatten
**Address:** 220 Stadium Boulevard
Singapore 397803 Singapore
**Phone:** +65 6344 7722

#153
## Cheok Kee Duck Rice
**Cuisines:** Asian Fusion
**Average price:** Under $10
**District:** Marine Parade
**Address:** 1220 East Coast Parkway
Singapore 468960 Singapore
**Phone:** +65 6445 4222

#154
## PS.Cafe Ann Siang
**Cuisines:** Modern European, Desserts
**Average price:** Above $61
**District:** Ann Siang Hill, Tanjong Pagar
**Address:** 45 Ann Siang Road
Singapore 069719 Singapore
**Phone:** +65 6222 3143

#155
## Food For Thought
**Cuisines:** Desserts, Asian, Burgers
**Average price:** $11-30
**District:** Bras Brasah
**Address:** 8 Queen Street
Singapore 188535 Singapore
**Phone:** +65 6338 9887

#156
## Food For Thought
**Cuisines:** Cafe
**Average price:** $11-30
**District:** Bukit Timah
**Address:** 1 Cluny Rd
Singapore 259569 Singapore
**Phone:** +65 6479 1080

#157
## East 8 New York Fusion
**Cuisines:** Tapas, Asian Fusion
**Average price:** $31-60
**District:** Bras Brasah, City Hall
**Address:** 10 Coleman Street
Singapore 179809 Singapore
**Phone:** +65 6338 8289

#158
## Da Paolo Pizzabar
**Cuisines:** Pizza, Italian
**Average price:** $11-30
**District:** Holland Village
**Address:** 44 Jalan Merah Saga
Singapore 278116 Singapore
**Phone:** +65 6479 6059

#159
## Beach Road Prawn Noodle House
**Cuisines:** Chinese, Street Vendors
**Average price:** Under $10
**District:** Siglap, Marine Parade
**Address:** 370 East Coast Road
Singapore 428981 Singapore
**Phone:** +65 6345 7196

#160
## Lolla
**Average price:** $31-60
**District:** Ann Siang Hill, Tanjong Pagar
**Address:** 22 Ann Siang Road
Singapore 069702 Singapore
**Phone:** +65 6423 1228

#161
## Cafe Melba
**Cuisines:** Cafe, Food
**Average price:** $11-30
**District:** Tanjong Rhu
**Address:** 90 Goodman Road
Singapore 439053 Singapore
**Phone:** +65 6440 6068

#162
## Restaurant Absinthe
**Cuisines:** French
**Average price:** Above $61
**District:** Boat Quay
**Address:** 72 Boat Quay
Singapore 049860 Singapore
**Phone:** +65 6222 9068

#163
## Real Food
**Cuisines:** Vegetarian
**Average price:** $11-30
**District:** Somerset
**Address:** 110 Killiney Road
Singapore 239549 Singapore
**Phone:** +65 6737 9516

#164
## Killiney Kopitiam
**Cuisines:** Breakfast & Brunch, Coffee & Tea
**Average price:** Under $10
**District:** Somerset
**Address:** 67 Killiney Road
Singapore 239525 Singapore
**Phone:** +65 6734 9648

#165
## Hediard French Cafe & Delicatessen Boutique
**Cuisines:** Cafe
**Average price:** $11-30
**District:** Tanglin
**Address:** 123 Tanglin Road
Singapore 247920 Singapore
**Phone:** +65 6333 6683

#166
## Wen Dao Shi
**Average price:** $11-30
**District:** Geylang
**Address:** 126 Sims Avenue
Singapore 387449 Singapore
**Phone:** +65 6746 4757

#167
## Eng Seng Restaurant
**Cuisines:** Chinese
**Average price:** $11-30
**District:** Joo Chiat
**Address:** 247/249 Joo Chiat Place
Singapore 427935 Singapore
**Phone:** +65 6440 5560

#168
## Fatboy's The Burger Bar
**Cuisines:** Burgers
**Average price:** $11-30
**District:** Joo Chiat
**Address:** 465 Joo Chiat Rd
Singapore 427677 Singapore
**Phone:** +65 6346 6081

#169
**Señor Taco**
**Cuisines:** Mexican
**Average price:** $11-30
**District:** Clarke Quay
**Address:** 3D River Valley Road
Singapore 179023 Singapore
**Phone:** +65 6337 1377

#170
**Ma Maison**
**Cuisines:** Japanese, French, Asian
**Average price:** $11-30
**District:** Bugis
**Address:** 200 Victoria Street Bugis
Junction, 188021 Singapore
**Phone:** +65 6338 4819

#171
**Freshly Baked by Le Bijoux**
**Cuisines:** Bakeries, Breakfast & Brunch
**Average price:** $11-30
**District:** Somerset, Orchard
**Address:** 57 Killiney Rd
Singapore 239520 Singapore
**Phone:** +65 6735 3298

#172
**PS.Cafe**
**Cuisines:** Cafe
**Average price:** $31-60
**District:** Tanglin
**Address:** 390 Orchard Road
Singapore 238871 Singapore
**Phone:** +65 6887 2207

#173
**Chikuwa Tei**
**Cuisines:** Japanese, Sushi Bar
**Average price:** $11-30
**District:** Robertson Quay
**Address:** 9 Mohamed Sultan Rd
Singapore 238959 Singapore
**Phone:** +65 6738 9395

#174
**La Petite Cuisine**
**Cuisines:** French
**Average price:** $11-30
**District:** Bukit Timah
**Address:** 10 Jalan Serene
Singapore 258748 Singapore
**Phone:** +65 6314 3173

#175
**Smokey's BBQ**
**Cuisines:** Barbeque
**Average price:** $31-60
**District:** Joo Chiat
**Address:** 73 Joo Chiat Pl
Singapore 427790 Singapore
**Phone:** +65 6345 6914

#176
**Alkaff Mansion Ristorante**
**Cuisines:** Italian, Mediterranean
**Average price:** $11-30
**District:** Telok Blangah
**Address:** 10 Telok Blangah Green
Singapore 109178 Singapore
**Phone:** +65 6510 3068

#177
**Ginza Bairin**
**Cuisines:** Japanese
**Average price:** $11-30
**District:** Robertson Quay
**Address:** 2 Orchard Turn, ION Orchard
Singapore 238801 Singapore
**Phone:** +65 6509 8101

#178
**&Made by Bruno Menard**
**Cuisines:** American
**Average price:** $31-60
**District:** Tanglin
**Address:** 9 Scotts Road
Singapore 228210 Singapore
**Phone:** +65 6732 9808

#179
**You Huak Restaurant:**
**Sembawang White Bee Hoon**
**Cuisines:** Chinese
**Average price:** Under $10
**District:** Sembawang, Yishun
**Address:** 22 Jalan Tampang
Singapore 758966 Singapore
**Phone:** +65 9843 4699

#180
**Napoleon Food & Wine Bar**
**Cuisines:** Modern European
**Average price:** $11-30
**District:** Tanjong Pagar
**Address:** 206 Telok Ayer Street
Singapore 068641 Singapore
**Phone:** +65 6221 9282

#181
**Spizza**
**Cuisines:** Pizza, Italian
**Average price:** $31-60
**District:** Raffles Place
**Address:** 29 Club Street
Singapore 069414 Singapore
**Phone:** +65 6224 2525

#182
**OTTO Ristorante**
**Cuisines:** Italian
**Average price:** Above $61
**District:** Tanjong Pagar
**Address:** Red Dot Design Museum 28
Maxwell Rd 069120 Singapore
**Phone:** +65 6227 6819

#183
**Hyangtogol Korean**
Cuisines: Korean
Average price: $11-30
District: Tanjong Pagar
Address: 165 Tanjong Pagar Road
Singapore 088539 Singapore
Phone: +65 6879 2555

#184
**Anjappar Authentic
Chenttinaad Restuarant**
Cuisines: Indian
Average price: $11-30
District: Little India, Farrer Park
Address: 76-78, Racecourse Rd
Singapore 218576 Singapore
Phone: +65 6296 5545

#185
**Founder Bak Kut Teh**
Cuisines: Grocery, Cafe
Average price: Under $10
District: Novena
Address: 347 Balestier Rd
Singapore 329777 Singapore
Phone: +65 6352 6192

#186
**Bruno's Pizzeria & Grill**
Cuisines: Italian, French, European
Average price: $11-30
District: Katong
Address: 338 Tanjong Katong Road
Singapore 437110 Singapore
Phone: +65 6440 4525

#187
**Privé**
Cuisines: American, Breakfast & Brunch
Average price: Above $61
District: Harbourfront
Address: No. 2 Keppel Bay Vista
Singapore 098382 Singapore
Phone: +65 6776 0777

#188
**Foo House**
Cuisines: Cafe
Average price: $11-30
District: Simei
Address: 6 Jalan Pari Burong
Singapore 488672 Singapore
Phone: +65 6445 3110

#189
**Hatched**
Average price: $11-30
District: Bukit Timah
Address: 01-06 Evans Lodge
Singapore 259367 Singapore
Phone: +65 6735 0012

#190
**Palm Beach Seafood**
Cuisines: Seafood, Chinese
Average price: Above $61
District: Bayfront, Raffles Place
Address: 1 Fullerton Road
Singapore 049213 Singapore
Phone: +65 6336 8118

#191
**Majestic Restaurant**
Cuisines: Asian Fusion, Chinese
Average price: $31-60
District: Chinatown
Address: 31 Bukit Pasoh Rd
Singapore 089845 Singapore
Phone: +65 6511 4718

#192
**De Classic Golden Spoon**
Cuisines: Asian Fusion
Average price: $11-30
District: Tiong Bahru
Address: 62 Seng Poh Lane
Singapore 160062 Singapore
Phone: +65 6536 2218

#193
**EspressoLab Singapore**
Cuisines: Coffee & Tea, Sandwiches
Average price: $11-30
District: Arab Street
Address: 13 Bali Lane
Singapore 189849 Singapore
Phone: +65 6298 8413

#194
**Da Lian Traditional Noodles**
Cuisines: Chinese
Average price: Under $10
District: Lavender
Address: 216G Syed Alwi Road
Singapore 207799 Singapore
Phone: +65 6396 3345

#195
**Ristorante Pietrasanta**
Cuisines: Italian, Diners, Pizza
Average price: $31-60
District: Wessex Estate
Address: 5B Portsdown Road
Singapore 139311 Singapore
Phone: +65 6479 9521

#196
**Penang Place Restaurant**
Cuisines: Buffets
Average price: $11-30
District: One-North
Address: 1 Fusionopolis Way,
Connexis #B1-20/24
Singapore 138632 Singapore
Phone: +65 6467 7003

#197
### Al Forno
**Cuisines:** Italian, Pizza
**Average price:** $11-30
**District:** Siglap, Marine Parade
**Address:** 400 East Coast Rd
Singapore 428996 Singapore
**Phone:** +65 6348 8781

#198
### Jai Thai
**Cuisines:** Thai
**Average price:** Under $10
**District:** Bishan
**Address:** 7 Clover Way
Singapore 579080 Singapore
**Phone:** +65 6258 0228

#199
### L'entrecote Bistro
**Cuisines:** French
**Average price:** $31-60
**District:** Duxton Hill, Tanjong Pagar
**Address:** 36 Duxton Hill
Singapore 089614 Singapore
**Phone:** +65 6238 5700

#200
### Victor's Kitchen
**Cuisines:** Dim Sum, Asian Fusion,
Breakfast & Brunch
**Average price:** $11-30
**District:** Bencoolen
**Address:** 91 Bencoolen Street
Singapore 189652 Singapore
**Phone:** +65 9838 2851

#201
### Peperoni Pizzeria
**Cuisines:** Pizza
**Average price:** $31-60
**District:** River Valley
**Address:** 56 Zion Road
Singapore 247781 Singapore
**Phone:** +65 6732 3253

#202
### La Maison Fatien
**Cuisines:** French
**Average price:** Above $61
**District:** Duxton Hill, Tanjong Pagar
**Address:** 76 Duxton Road
Singapore 089535 Singapore
**Phone:** +65 6220 3822

#203
### Paulaner Bräuhaus Singapore
**Cuisines:** Bars, Cafe
**Average price:** $11-30
**District:** City Hall
**Address:** 9 Raffles Boulevard
Singapore 039596 Singapore
**Phone:** +65 6883 2572

#204
### Sapporo Ramen Miharu
**Cuisines:** Japanese
**Average price:** $11-30
**District:** Robertson Quay
**Address:** 1 Nanson Road
Singapore 238909 Singapore
**Phone:** +65 6733 8464

#205
### Z'en Japanese Cuisine
**Cuisines:** Buffets, Japanese
**Average price:** $11-30
**District:** Robertson Quay
**Address:** 207 River Valley Road
Singapore 238275 Singapore
**Phone:** +65 6732 3110

#206
### Por Kee Eating House
**Cuisines:** Chinese
**Average price:** $11-30
**District:** Tiong Bahru
**Address:** 69 Seng Poh Lane
Singapore 160069 Singapore
**Phone:** +65 6221 0582

#207
### Jollibee
**Cuisines:** Filipino, Fast Food
**Average price:** Under $10
**District:** Orchard
**Address:** 304 Orchard Road
Singapore 238863 Singapore
**Phone:** +65 6735 5117

#208
### VeganBurg
**Cuisines:** Fast Food, Vegetarian,
Burgers
**Average price:** $11-30
**District:** Bayfront
**Address:** 44 Jalan Eunos
Singapore 419502 Singapore
**Phone:** +65 6844 6868

#209
### Prego
**Cuisines:** French, Italian, Mediterranean
**Average price:** Above $61
**District:** Bras Brasah, City Hall
**Address:** 1F Fairmont Singapore,
80 Bras Basah Road
Singapore 189560 Singapore
**Phone:** +65 6431 6156

#210
### Bistro du Vin
**Cuisines:** French
**Average price:** Above $61
**District:** Tanglin
**Address:** 1 Scotts Road
Singapore 358666 Singapore
**Phone:** +65 6733 7763

#211
**Upper Crust**
**Cuisines:** Sandwiches
**Average price:** $11-30
**District:** Raffles Place
**Address:** 1 Raffles Place
Singapore 048616 Singapore
**Phone:** +65 6536 3138

#212
**Shinzo Japanese Cuisine**
**Cuisines:** Japanese, Sushi Bar
**Average price:** Above $61
**District:** Clarke Quay
**Address:** 17 Carpenter Street
Singapore 059906 Singapore
**Phone:** +65 6438 2921

#213
**Patisserie Glace**
**Cuisines:** Japanese, Bakeries
**Average price:** $11-30
**District:** Tanjong Pagar
**Address:** 12 Gopeng Street
Singapore 078877 Singapore
**Phone:** +65 6400 0247

#214
**La Dolce Vita**
**Cuisines:** Italian
**Average price:** $31-60
**District:** City Hall
**Address:** 5 Raffles Avenue
Singapore 039797 Singapore
**Phone:** +65 6885 3551

#215
**Nirai Kanai Okinawan Restaurant**
**Cuisines:** Japanese
**Average price:** $11-30
**District:** Clarke Quay
**Address:** 177 River Valley Road,
#B1-01/02 Singapore 179030 Singapore
**Phone:** +65 6339 4811

#216
**Hood Bar and Cafe**
**Cuisines:** Bars, Cafe
**Average price:** $11-30
**District:** Bugis
**Address:** 201 Victoria Street
Singapore 188067 Singapore
**Phone:** +65 6221 8846

#217
**Romankan Yokohama**
**Cuisines:** Fast Food, Japanese
**Average price:** Under $10
**District:** Orchard
**Address:** Ngee Ann City, 391
Orchard Road, 238872 Singapore
**Phone:** +65 6738 2505

#218
**Mei Heong Yuen Dessert**
**Cuisines:** Desserts, Chinese
**Average price:** $11-30
**District:** Orchard
**Address:** 2 Orchard Turn
Singapore 238801 Singapore
**Phone:** +65 6509 3301

#219
**Hong Kong Street Family
Restaurant**
**Cuisines:** Cantonese
**Average price:** $11-30
**District:** Newton, Novena
**Address:** 273 Thomson Road
Singapore 307644 Singapore
**Phone:** +65 6252 3132

#220
**Boon Tong Kee**
**Cuisines:** Chinese
**Average price:** $11-30
**District:** Boon Keng
**Address:** 34 Whampoa West
Singapore 330034 Singapore
**Phone:** +65 6299 9880

#221
**Spize Supper Club**
**Cuisines:** Asian Fusion
**Average price:** $11-30
**District:** Simei
**Address:** 336/338 Bedok Road
Singapore 469516 Singapore
**Phone:** +65 6445 3211

#222
**Loy Kee Best Chicken Rice**
**Cuisines:** Chinese
**Average price:** $11-30
**District:** Novena
**Address:** 342 Balestier Road
Singapore 329774 Singapore
**Phone:** +65 6252 2318

#223
**Open Door Policy**
**Cuisines:** Cafe
**Average price:** Above $61
**District:** Tiong Bahru
**Address:** 19 Yong Siak St
Singapore 168650 Singapore
**Phone:** +65 6221 9307

#224
**LeVeL33**
**Cuisines:** Bars, Gastropubs
**Average price:** $31-60
**District:** Bayfront
**Address:** 8 Marina Boulevard #33-01
Singapore 018981 Singapore
**Phone:** +65 6834 3133

#225
**Kith Cafe**
**Cuisines:** Cafe, Breakfast & Brunch
**Average price:** $11-30
**District:** Dhoby Ghaut, Orchard
**Address:** 9 Penang Road
Singapore 238459 Singapore
**Phone:** +65 6338 8611

#226
**Paul Bakery**
**Cuisines:** French, Coffee & Tea
**Average price:** $31-60
**District:** Orchard
**Address:** 391A Orchard Road
Singapore 238873 Singapore
**Phone:** +65 6836 5932

#227
**Cocotte**
**Cuisines:** French
**Average price:** Above $61
**District:** Little India
**Address:** 2 Dickson Road
Singapore 209494 Singapore
**Phone:** +44 6298 1198

#228
**Nassim Hill**
**Cuisines:** Bars, Cafe, Bakeries
**Average price:** $11-30
**District:** Tanglin
**Address:** 56 Tanglin Road #01-03
Tanglin Post Office Singapore 247964
**Phone:** +65 6835 1128

#229
**Spr.Mkrt**
**Cuisines:** Breakfast & Brunch
**Average price:** $11-30
**District:** Tanjong Pagar
**Address:** 2 Mccallum Street
Singapore 069043 Singapore
**Phone:** +65 6221 2105

#230
**Ayam Penyet Ria**
**Cuisines:** Indonesian
**Average price:** Under $10
**District:** Orchard
**Address:** 304 Orchard Road
Singapore 238863 Singapore
**Phone:** +65 6235 6390

#231
**First Thai Food**
**Cuisines:** Thai
**Average price:** $11-30
**District:** Bugis, Bras Brasah, City Hall
**Address:** 23 Purvis St
Singapore 188600 Singapore
**Phone:** +65 6339 3123

#232
**The Line**
**Cuisines:** American, Buffets
**Average price:** Above $61
**District:** Tanglin
**Address:** 22 Orange Grove Rd
Singapore 258350 Singapore
**Phone:** +65 6213 4275

#233
**Bincho at Hua Bee**
**Cuisines:** Japanese
**Average price:** $11-30
**District:** Tiong Bahru
**Address:** 78 Moh Guan Terrace
Singapore 162078 Singapore
**Phone:** +65 6438 4567

#234
**Geisha Specialty Coffee**
**Cuisines:** Cafe
**Average price:** Under $10
**District:** Bencoolen
**Address:** 175 Bencoolen Street
Singapore 189649 Singapore
**Phone:** +65 9062 5726

#235
**Khansama Tandoori**
**Cuisines:** Indian
**Average price:** $31-60
**District:** Little India
**Address:** 166 Serangoon Rd
Singapore 218050 Singapore
**Phone:** +65 6299 0300

#236
**Roadhouse**
**Cuisines:** American, Burgers
**Average price:** $31-60
**District:** Queenstown, Dempsey Hill
**Address:** 13 Dempsey Road
Singapore 249674 Singapore
**Phone:** +65 6476 2922

#237
**Summer Palace**
**Cuisines:** Cantonese
**Average price:** Above $61
**District:** Tanglin
**Address:** 1 Cuscaden Road
Singapore 249715 Singapore
**Phone:** +65 6725 3288

#238
**Wee Nam Kee Chicken Rice**
**Cuisines:** Chinese
**Average price:** Under $10
**District:** Novena
**Address:** 101 Thomson Road
Singapore 307591 Singapore
**Phone:** +65 6255 6396

#239
## Two Chefs Eating Place
**Cuisines:** Chinese
**Average price:** $11-30
**District:** Holland Hill
**Address:** 116 Commonwealth Crescent
Singapore 140116 Singapore
**Phone:** +65 6472 5361

#240
## Hup Choon Eating House
**Average price:** $31-60
**District:** Bukit Timah
**Address:** 1 Binjai Park
Singapore 589818 Singapore
**Phone:** +65 6468 4081

#241
## Sauce
**Cuisines:** FastFood
**Average price:** $11-30
**District:** Bayfront, City Hall
**Address:** 8 Raffles Avenue
Singapore 039802 Singapore
**Phone:** +65 6837 2959

#242
## Greenwood Fish Market & Bistro
**Cuisines:** Seafood, Seafood Markets
**Average price:** $11-30
**District:** Bukit Timah
**Address:** 34 Greenwood Avenue
Singapore 289236 Singapore
**Phone:** +65 6467 4950

#243
## Alif
**Average price:** Under $10
**District:** Bukit Batok
**Address:** 01-204 374 Bukit Batok St 31
Singapore 650374 Singapore
**Phone:** +65 6564 6324

#244
## Blu Jaz Cafe
**Cuisines:** Cafe
**Average price:** $11-30
**District:** Arab Street
**Address:** 11 Bali Lane
Singapore 189848 Singapore
**Phone:** +65 6292 3800

#245
## Timbre Substation
**Average price:** $11-30
**District:** Bras Brasah, Dhoby Ghaut
**Address:** 45 Armenian Street
Singapore 179936 Singapore
**Phone:** +65 6338 8030

#246
## The Manhattan Pizza Co.
**Cuisines:** Pizza
**Average price:** Under $10
**District:** Somerset, Orchard
**Address:** 181 Orchard Road
Singapore 329141 Singapore
**Phone:** +65 6238 8229

#247
## Boon Tong Kee
**Cuisines:** Chinese
**Average price:** Under $10
**District:** Novena
**Address:** 399, 401 & 403 Balestier Rd
Singapore 329801 Singapore
**Phone:** +65 6254 3937

#248
## Extra Virgin Pizza
**Cuisines:** Pizza
**Average price:** $11-30
**District:** Bayfront, Raffles Place
**Address:** 8 Marina View
Singapore 018960 Singapore
**Phone:** +65 6247 5757

#249
## Inle Myanmar
**Cuisines:** Asian Fusion, Burmese
**Average price:** Under $10
**District:** Bras Brasah, City Hall
**Address:** 111 North Bridge Rd
Singapore 179098 Singapore
**Phone:** +65 6333 5438

#250
## Cherry Garden
**Average price:** Above $61
**District:** City Hall
**Address:** 5 Raffles Ave
Singapore 039797 Singapore
**Phone:** +65 6885 3538

#251
## Chin Chin Restaurant
**Cuisines:** Chinese, Coffee & Tea
**Average price:** Under $10
**District:** Bugis, Bras Brasah, City Hall
**Address:** 19 Purvis Street
Singapore 188598 Singapore
**Phone:** +65 6337 4640

#252
## Crystal Jade Golden Palace
**Average price:** $11-30
**District:** Orchard
**Address:** 290 Orchard Road
Singapore 238859 Singapore
**Phone:** +65 6734 6866

#253
**East Ocean Teochew**
**Cuisines:** Dim Sum
**Average price:** $11-30
**District:** Orchard
**Address:** 391 Orchard Road
Singapore 238872 Singapore
**Phone:** +65 6235 9088

#254
**The Magic of Chongqing Hot Pot**
**Cuisines:** Chinese
**Average price:** $11-30
**District:** Tanglin
**Address:** 19 Tanglin Road
Singapore 247909 Singapore
**Phone:** +65 6734 8135

#255
**Patara Fine Thai Cuisine**
**Cuisines:** Thai
**Average price:** $11-30
**District:** Tanglin
**Address:** 163 Tanglin Road
Singapore 247933 Singapore
**Phone:** +65 6737 0818

#256
**Rakuichi**
**Cuisines:** Japanese, Sushi Bar
**Average price:** Above $61
**District:** Queenstown, Dempsey Hill
**Address:** 10 Dempsey Rd
Singapore 247700 Singapore
**Phone:** +65 6474 2143

#257
**Thunder Tea Rice**
**Cuisines:** Chinese
**Average price:** Under $10
**District:** Joo Chiat
**Address:** 328 Joo Chiat Road
Singapore 427585 Singapore
**Phone:** +65 6342 0023

#258
**The Curry Wok**
**Cuisines:** Chinese
**Average price:** $11-30
**District:** Bukit Timah
**Address:** 5 Coronation Rd
Singapore 269406 Singapore
**Phone:** +65 6464 8878

#259
**Sabio Tapas Bar**
**Cuisines:** Spanish, Bar
**Average price:** Above $61
**District:** Duxton Hill, Tanjong Pagar
**Address:** 5 Duxton Hill
Singapore 089591 Singapore
**Phone:** +65 6690 7562

#260
**Sun Japanese Dining**
**Cuisines:** Desserts, Sushi Bar
**Average price:** $11-30
**District:** Bras Brasah
**Address:** 30 Victoria St
Singapore 187996 Singapore
**Phone:** +65 6336 3166

#261
**Antoinette**
**Cuisines:** French, Bakeries, Desserts
**Average price:** $31-60
**District:** Lavender
**Address:** 30 Penhas Road
Singapore 208188 Singapore
**Phone:** +65 6293 3121

#262
**Wrap & Roll**
**Cuisines:** Vietnamese
**Average price:** Under $10
**District:** One-North
**Address:** 1 Vista Exchange Green
Singapore 138617 Singapore
**Phone:** +65 6694 4111

#263
**Au Petit Salut**
**Cuisines:** French
**Average price:** $31-60
**District:** Queenstown, Dempsey Hill
**Address:** 40c Harding Rd
Singapore 249548 Singapore
**Phone:** +65 6475 1976

#264
**Sin Huat Seafood Restaurant**
**Cuisines:** Seafood
**Average price:** Above $61
**District:** Geylang
**Address:** 659/661 Geylang Rd
Singapore 389589 Singapore
**Phone:** +65 6744 9755

#265
**Brasserie Gavroche**
**Cuisines:** French, Brasseries
**Average price:** $11-30
**District:** Tanjong Pagar
**Address:** 66 Tras Street
Singapore 079005 Singapore
**Phone:** +65 6225 8266

#266
**Santaro @ Hinoki Japanese Restaurant**
**Cuisines:** Japanese, Sushi Bar
**Average price:** $31-60
**District:** Raffles Place
**Address:** 22 Cross Street
Singapore 048421 Singapore
**Phone:** +65 6536 7746

#267
## Melt - The World Cafe
**Cuisines:** Buffets
**Average price:** Above $61
**District:** City Hall
**Address:** 5 Raffles Avenue
Singapore 039797 Singapore
**Phone:** +65 6885 3082

#268
## Ramen Santouka
**Cuisines:** Japanese
**Average price:** $11-30
**District:** Somerset, Orchard
**Address:** 21 Cuppage Road
Singapore 229452 Singapore
**Phone:** +65 6235 1059

#269
## Huber's Butchery and Bistro
**Cuisines:** Butcher
**Average price:** $11-30
**District:** Queenstown, Dempsey Hill
**Address:** 18A & 18B Dempsey Road
Singapore 249677 Singapore
**Phone:** +65 6737 1588

#270
## Keng Eng Kee Seafood
**Cuisines:** Seafood
**Average price:** $11-30
**District:** Alexandra
**Address:** 124 Bukit Merah Lane 1
Singapore 150124 Singapore
**Phone:** +65 6272 1038

#271
## Hua Yu Wee
**Average price:** $31-60
**District:** Bedok South
**Address:** 462 Upper East Coast Rd
Singapore 466508 Singapore
**Phone:** +65 6442 9313

#272
## Ban Leong Wah Hoe Seafood
**Cuisines:** Seafood
**Average price:** $11-30
**District:** Thomson
**Address:** 122 Casuarina Rd
Singapore 579510 Singapore
**Phone:** +65 6452 2824

#273
## Auntie Kim's Korean Restaurant
**Cuisines:** Korean
**Average price:** $11-30
**District:** Thomson
**Address:** 265 Upper Thomson Rd
Singapore 574392 Singapore
**Phone:** +65 6452 2112

#274
## Brotzeit
**Cuisines:** German, Breweries, Modern European
**Average price:** $11-30
**District:** Bras Brasah, City Hall
**Address:** 252 North Bridge Road
Singapore 179103 Singapore
**Phone:** +65 6883 1534

#275
## The White Rabbit
**Cuisines:** Bars, Modern European
**Average price:** $31-60
**District:** Queenstown
**Address:** 39C Harding Rd
Singapore 249541 Singapore
**Phone:** +65 9721 0536

#276
## Jing
**Cuisines:** Chinese
**Average price:** $11-30
**District:** Bayfront, Raffles Place
**Address:** 1 Fullerton Rd
Singapore 049213 Singapore
**Phone:** +65 6224 0088

#277
## Zhong Hua Steamboat
**Cuisines:** Chinese
**Average price:** $11-30
**District:** Bugis, City Hall
**Address:** 95 Beach Road 01-01
Singapore 189699 Singapore
**Phone:** +65 6337 1655

#278
## Red House at The Quayside
**Cuisines:** Seafood
**Average price:** $31-60
**District:** Robertson Quay
**Address:** Robertson Quay 60
Singapore 238252 Singapore
**Phone:** +65 6735 7666

#279
## Ichiban Boshi
**Cuisines:** Japanese
**Average price:** $31-60
**District:** Somerset, Orchard
**Address:** Orchard Rd 176
Singapore 238843 Singapore
**Phone:** +65 6737 7232

#280
## Yakinikutei Ao-Chan
**Cuisines:** Japanese, Professional Services
**Average price:** $11-30
**District:** Dhoby Ghaut, Orchard
**Address:** 100 Orchard Rd
Singapore 238840 Singapore
**Phone:** +65 6735 6457

#281
### Hashida Sushi
**Cuisines:** Japanese, Sushi Bar
**Average price:** Above $61
**District:** Somerset, Orchard
**Address:** 333A Orchard Road
Singapore 238897 Singapore
**Phone:** +65 6733 2114

#282
### RM Minang House
**Cuisines:** Indonesian
**Average price:** $11-30
**District:** Orchard
**Address:** 304 Orchard Road Singapore
**Phone:** +65 6887 4702

#283
### The Rice Table
**Cuisines:** Indonesian
**Average price:** $11-30
**District:** Tanglin
**Address:** 360 Orchard Rd
Singapore 238869 Singapore
**Phone:** +65 6835 3783

#284
### Susan Chan Food
**Average price:** $11-30
**District:** Orchard
**Address:** 14 Scotts Road
Singapore 228213 Singapore
**Phone:** +65 6733 5953

#285
### The Cliff at Sentosa
**Cuisines:** Modern European
**Average price:** $11-30
**District:** Sentosa
**Address:** 2 Bukit Manis
Singapore 099891 Singapore
**Phone:** +65 6371 1425

#286
### Da Paolo Ristorante
**Cuisines:** Italian
**Average price:** $31-60
**District:** Holland Village
**Address:** 43 Jalan Merah Saga
Singapore 278116 Singapore
**Phone:** +65 6476 1332

#287
### Ban Mian Stall Jun Hang Food Court
**Cuisines:** Chinese, Taiwanese
**Average price:** Under $10
**District:** Clementi
**Address:** 461 Clementi Road
Singapore 599491 Singapore
**Phone:** +65 6465 1191

#288
### Botak Jones
**Cuisines:** American
**Average price:** $11-30
**District:** Clementi, West Coast
**Address:** Block 325 Clementi Avenue 5
Singapore 120325 Singapore
**Phone:** +65 6774 1225

#289
### 2D1N Souju Bang
**Cuisines:** Korean
**Average price:** $11-30
**District:** Duxton Hill, Tanjong Pagar
**Address:** 44/46 Tanjong Pagar Rd
Singapore 088465 Singapore
**Phone:** +65 6227 6033

#290
### Spathe Public House
**Cuisines:** Bistro
**Average price:** $11-30
**District:** Robertson Quay
**Address:** 8 Mohamed Sultan Road
Singapore 238958 Singapore
**Phone:** +65 6735 1035

#291
### The Lawn Salad & Grill Cafe
**Cuisines:** Cafe, Salad
**Average price:** Under $10
**District:** One-North
**Address:** 31 Biopolis Way
Singapore 138669 Singapore
**Phone:** +65 6478 9739

#292
### Arbite
**Cuisines:** Food, Breakfast & Brunch
**Average price:** $11-30
**District:** Serangoon Gardens
**Address:** 66A Serangoon Garden Way
Singapore 555962 Singapore
**Phone:** +65 6287 0430

#293
### Porta Porta Italian
**Cuisines:** Modern European, Italian
**Average price:** Above $61
**District:** Changi
**Address:** 971C Upper Changi Rd North
Singapore 507668 Singapore
**Phone:** +65 6545 3108

#294
### Boon Tong Kee
**Cuisines:** Chinese
**Average price:** Under $10
**District:** River Valley
**Address:** 425 River Valley Rd
Singapore 248324 Singapore
**Phone:** +65 6736 3213

#295
**Momiji Japanese Buffet Restaurant**
**Cuisines:** Japanese
**Average price:** $31-60
**District:** Yishun
**Address:** 930 Yishun Ave 2 #03-47/50
Singapore 768098 Singapore
**Phone:** +65 6484 1090

#296
**Changi Village**
**Cuisines:** Ethnic Food, Pubs, Asian Fusion
**Average price:** $11-30
**District:** Changi
**Address:** 1 Netheravon Road
Singapore 508502 Singapore
**Phone:** +65 6379 7111

#297
**Ikeikemaru Ryoshi Sushi**
**Cuisines:** Japanese, Sushi Bar
**Average price:** $11-30
**District:** Clarke Quay
**Address:** 177 River Valley Road
Singapore 179030 Singapore
**Phone:** +65 6337 1022

#298
**No Signboard Seafood**
**Cuisines:** Seafood
**Average price:** $31-60
**District:** Harbourfront
**Address:** 1 Harbourfront Walk
Singapore 098585 Singapore
**Phone:** +65 6376 9959

#299
**Nam Nam Noodle Bar**
**Cuisines:** Vietnamese
**Average price:** Under $10
**District:** Bras Brasah, City Hall
**Address:** 252 North Bridge Road
Singapore 179103 Singapore
**Phone:** +65 6336 0500

#300
**Garibaldi Italian Restaurant & Bar**
**Cuisines:** Bars, Italian, European
**Average price:** Above $61
**District:** Bugis, Bras Brasah, City Hall
**Address:** 36 Purvis Street
Singapore 188613 Singapore
**Phone:** +65 6837 1468

#301
**Fika**
**Cuisines:** Cafe
**Average price:** $11-30
**District:** Arab Street
**Address:** 257 Beach Road
Singapore 199539 Singapore
**Phone:** +65 6396 9096

#302
**Fordham & Grand**
**Cuisines:** Bar
**Average price:** $11-30
**District:** Tanjong Pagar
**Address:** 43 Craig Road
Singapore 089681 Singapore
**Phone:** +65 6221 3088

#303
**Bibigo**
**Cuisines:** Korean
**Average price:** Under $10
**District:** Bras Brasah, City Hall
**Address:** 252 North Bridge Road
Singapore 179103 Singapore
**Phone:** +65 6336 4745

#304
**Sushi Tei**
**Cuisines:** Japanese
**Average price:** $31-60
**District:** Bras Brasah, City Hall
**Address:** 252 North Bridge Road
Singapore 179103 Singapore
**Phone:** +65 6334 7887

#305
**The Merry Men**
**Cuisines:** American, Breakfast & Brunch
**Average price:** $11-30
**District:** Robertson Quay
**Address:** 86 Robertson Quay
Singapore 238245 Singapore
**Phone:** +65 6735 9667

#306
**Boomarang Bistro & Bar**
**Cuisines:** Bars, Breakfast & Brunch
**Average price:** $11-30
**District:** Robertson Quay
**Address:** 01-15 The Quayside
Singapore 238252 Singapore
**Phone:** +65 6738 1077

#307
**Big Mama**
**Cuisines:** Korean
**Average price:** $11-30
**District:** Tiong Bahru
**Address:** 2 Kim Tian Road
Singapore 169244 Singapore
**Phone:** +65 6270 7704

#308
**CM-PB Contemporary Melting-Pot & Bar**
**Cuisines:** Asian Fusion
**Average price:** $31-60
**District:** Queenstown, Dempsey Hill
**Address:** Block 7 Dempsey Road
Singapore 249671 Singapore
**Phone:** +65 6475 0105

#309
## House
**Cuisines:** Asian Fusion, American
**Average price:** $11-30
**District:** Queenstown, Dempsey Hill
**Address:** 8D Dempsey Road
Singapore 249672 Singapore
**Phone:** +65 6475 7787

#310
## La Nonna
**Cuisines:** Italian
**Average price:** $31-60
**District:** Bukit Timah
**Address:** 76 Namly Pl
Singapore 267226 Singapore
**Phone:** +65 6762 1587

#311
## Yhingthai Palace
**Cuisines:** Thai
**Average price:** $31-60
**District:** Bugis, Bras Brasah, City Hall
**Address:** 36 Purvis Street
Singapore 188613 Singapore
**Phone:** +65 6337 9429

#312
## Dessert Bowl
**Cuisines:** Cafe
**Average price:** Under $10
**District:** Serangoon Gardens
**Address:** 80A Serangoon Garden Way
Singapore 555976 Singapore
**Phone:** +65 6285 1278

#313
## Real Food
**Cuisines:** Fruits & Veggies, Vegetarian
**Average price:** $11-30
**District:** Clarke Quay
**Address:** 6 Eu Tong Seng Street
Singapore 059817 Singapore
**Phone:** +65 6224 4492

#314
## The Flying Squirrel
**Cuisines:** Cafe
**Average price:** $11-30
**District:** Tanjong Pagar
**Address:** 92 Amoy Street
Singapore 069911 Singapore
**Phone:** +65 6226 2203

#315
## Les Bouchons
**Cuisines:** Steakhouses
**Average price:** $31-60
**District:** Ann Siang Hill, Tanjong Pagar
**Address:** 7 Ann Siang Road
Singapore 069689 Singapore
**Phone:** +65 6423 0737

#316
## L'angelus
**Cuisines:** French
**Average price:** Above $61
**District:** Ann Siang Hill, Tanjong Pagar
**Address:** 85 Club Street
Singapore 069453 Singapore
**Phone:** +65 6225 6897

#317
## Lan Zhou La Mian
**Cuisines:** Chinese
**Average price:** $11-30
**District:** Chinatown
**Address:** 19 Smith Street
Singapore 058933 Singapore
**Phone:** +65 6327 1286

#318
## Mikuni
**Cuisines:** Japanese
**Average price:** Above $61
**District:** Bras Brasah, City Hall
**Address:** 80 Bras Basah Road
Singapore 189560 Singapore
**Phone:** +65 6431 6156

#319
## Dozo Restaurant
**Cuisines:** Japanese
**Average price:** Above $61
**District:** River Valley
**Address:** 491 River Valley Rd
Singapore 248371 Singapore
**Phone:** +65 6838 6966

#320
## Imperial Treasure Noodle & Congee House
**Cuisines:** Fast Food
**Average price:** $11-30
**District:** Orchard
**Address:** 2 Orchard Turn
Singapore 238801 Singapore
**Phone:** +65 6509 8283

#321
## Yantra
**Cuisines:** Indian
**Average price:** $31-60
**District:** Tanglin
**Address:** 163 Tanglin Road
Singapore 247933 Singapore
**Phone:** +65 6836 3112

#322
## La Ristrettos
**Cuisines:** Cafe, Coffee & Tea
**Average price:** $11-30
**District:** Novena
**Address:** 10 Sinaran Drive Novena
Medical Centre 307506 Singapore
**Phone:** +65 6397 7165

#323
## Urban Bites Mediterranean Cuisine
**Cuisines:** Mediterranean, Cafe
**Average price:** $11-30
**District:** Tanjong Pagar
**Address:** 161 Telok Ayer Street
Singapore 068615 Singapore
**Phone:** +65 6327 9460

#324
## Noti Restaurant & Bar
**Cuisines:** Italian
**Average price:** Above $61
**District:** Ann Siang Hill, Tanjong Pagar
**Address:** 54 & 56 Club Street
Singapore 069430 Singapore
**Phone:** +65 6222 0089

#325
## Chili's
**Cuisines:** Fast Food
**Average price:** $11-30
**District:** Raffles Place
**Address:** 26 Sentosa Gateway
Singapore 098138 Singapore
**Phone:** +65 6733 3317

#326
## Heng Kee Curry Chicken Mee
**Average price:** $11-30
**District:** Chinatown
**Address:** 531a Upper Cross Street
Singapore 051531 Singapore
**Phone:** +65 6535 1077

#327
## Jang Won Korean
**Cuisines:** Korean
**Average price:** $11-30
**District:** Chinatown
**Address:** 44 Mosque St
Singapore 059522 Singapore
**Phone:** +65 6532 6949

#328
## A-Roy Thai
**Cuisines:** Thai
**Average price:** $31-60
**District:** City Hall
**Address:** 109 North Bridge Road
Singapore 179097 Singapore
**Phone:** +65 6388 3880

#329
## Szechuan Court & Kitchen
**Cuisines:** Szechuan
**Average price:** $11-30
**District:** Bras Brasah, City Hall
**Address:** 80 Bras Basah Road
Singapore 189560 Singapore
**Phone:** +65 6339 7777

#330
## The Halia At Raffles Hotel
**Cuisines:** Cocktail Bars, Asian Fusion
**Average price:** $31-60
**District:** Bras Brasah, City Hall
**Address:** 1 Beach Road
Singapore 189673 Singapore
**Phone:** +65 9639 1148

#331
## Fandango Tapas & Wine Bar
**Cuisines:** Bars, Tapas
**Average price:** Above $61
**District:** Bras Brasah
**Address:** 30 Victoria Street
Singapore 187996 Singapore
**Phone:** +65 6333 3450

#332
## Victory Restaurant Pte. Ltd
**Cuisines:** Indian
**Average price:** Under $10
**District:** Arab Street
**Address:** 701 North Bridge Road
Singapore 198677 Singapore
**Phone:** +65 6298 6955

#333
## Imperial Treasure Nan Bei Restaurant
**Cuisines:** Chinese
**Average price:** $11-30
**District:** Orchard
**Address:** 391 Orchard Road
Singapore 238872 Singapore
**Phone:** +65 6738 1238

#334
## Angus Steak House
**Cuisines:** Steakhouses
**Average price:** Above $61
**District:** Orchard
**Address:** 391 Orchard Road
Singapore 238872 Singapore
**Phone:** +65 6735 6015

#335
## Murugan Idli Shop
**Cuisines:** Indian
**Average price:** Under $10
**District:** Little India
**Address:** 81 Syed Alwi Rd
Singapore 207660 Singapore
**Phone:** +65 6298 0858

#336
## Ah Loy Thai
**Cuisines:** Thai
**Average price:** $11-30
**District:** Tampines
**Address:** 4 Tampines Central 5
Singapore 529510 Singapore
**Phone:** +65 9165 1543

#337
## Sopra Cucina & Bar
**Cuisines:** Italian
**Average price:** $31-60
**District:** Tanglin
**Address:** 10 Claymore Road
Singapore 229540 Singapore
**Phone:** +65 6737 3253

#338
## La Forketta
**Cuisines:** Italian
**Average price:** $11-30
**District:** Tanglin
**Address:** 1 Nassim Road
Singapore 258458 Singapore
**Phone:** +65 6836 3373

#339
## Muddy Murphy's
**Cuisines:** Pubs, Irish
**Average price:** $11-30
**District:** Tanglin
**Address:** 111 Somerset Road
Singapore 238879 Singapore
**Phone:** +65 6735 0400

#340
## Blue Bali on Cluny
**Cuisines:** Indonesian
**Average price:** $31-60
**District:** Bukit Timah
**Address:** House 1D Cluny Road
Singapore 259600 Singapore
**Phone:** +65 6733 0185

#341
## Bistro One Zero Three
**Cuisines:** Bistro
**Average price:** $11-30
**District:** Pasir Panjang
**Address:** 103 Pasir Panjang Rd
Singapore 118531 Singapore
**Phone:** +65 6476 6373

#342
## Fatboy's The Burger Bar
**Cuisines:** Burgers
**Average price:** $11-30
**District:** Pasir Panjang
**Address:** 122 Pasir Panjang Rd
Singapore 118544 Singapore
**Phone:** +65 6471 3224

#343
## Teck Teochew Porridge
**Cuisines:** Teochew
**Average price:** $11-30
**District:** Joo Chiat
**Address:** 128 Tembeling Road
Singapore 423638 Singapore
**Phone:** +65 9880 7932

#344
## Fratini La Trattoria
**Cuisines:** Italian
**Average price:** $11-30
**District:** Bukit Timah
**Address:** 10 Greenwood Avenue
Singapore 289201 Singapore
**Phone:** +65 6468 2868

#345
## Ootoya
**Cuisines:** Japanese
**Average price:** $11-30
**District:** Clementi, West Coast
**Address:** 3155 Commonwealth Avenue
West Clementi 12, 129588 Singapore
**Phone:** +65 6659 2644

#346
## Necessary Provisions
**Cuisines:** Coffee & Tea, Bistro
**Average price:** $11-30
**District:** Upper Bukit Timah
**Address:** 21 Eng Kong Terrace
Singapore 598993 Singapore
**Phone:** +65 9231 7920

#347
## Thien Kee Steamboat Restaurant
**Cuisines:** Chinese
**Average price:** $11-30
**District:** Arab Street
**Address:** 6001 Beach Road
Singapore 199589 Singapore
**Phone:** +65 6298 5891

#348
## Hombre Cantina
**Cuisines:** Mexican, Bar
**Average price:** $11-30
**District:** Boat Quay
**Address:** 53 Boat Quay
Singapore 049842 Singapore
**Phone:** +65 6438 6708

#349
## Flutes
**Cuisines:** Modern European
**Average price:** Above $61
**District:** Dhoby Ghaut
**Address:** 93 Stamford Road, #01-02
Singapore 178897 Singapore
**Phone:** +65 6338 8770

#350
## Sik Wai Sin Eating House - Cantonese Tze Char
**Average price:** $11-30
**District:** Kallang, Geylang
**Address:** 287 Geylang Rd
Singapore 389334 Singapore
**Phone:** +65 6744 0129

#351
## Wahiro Boutique Japanese
**Cuisines:** Japanese
**Average price:** $11-30
**District:** Marine Parade, Katong
**Address:** 50 East Coast Rd
Singapore 428769 Singapore
**Phone:** +65 6342 2252

#352
## Soup Restaurant
**Cuisines:** Chinese
**Average price:** $11-30
**District:** Tampines
**Address:** 2 Tampines Central 5,
Century Square, 529509 Singapore
**Phone:** +65 6781 8885

#353
## Tian Tian Hainanese
**Average price:** $11-30
**District:** Joo Chiat
**Address:** 443 Joo Chiat Road
Singapore 427656 Singapore
**Phone:** +65 6345 9443

#354
## Thohirah Restaurant
**Cuisines:** Asian Fusion
**Average price:** Under $10
**District:** Yio Chu Kang
**Address:** 258 Jalan Kayu
Singapore 799487 Singapore
**Phone:** +65 6481 2009

#355
## Geylang Lorong 29 Hokkien Mee
**Cuisines:** Vietnamese
**Average price:** $11-30
**District:** Siglap, Marine Parade
**Address:** 396 East Coast Road
Singapore 428994 Singapore
**Phone:** +65 6242 0080

#356
## Fatboy's The Burger Bar
**Cuisines:** Bars, Burgers
**Average price:** $11-30
**District:** Thomson
**Address:** 187 Upper Thomson Rd
Singapore 574335 Singapore
**Phone:** +65 6252 8780

#357
## Kko Kko Na Ra
**Cuisines:** Korean
**Average price:** $11-30
**District:** Tanjong Pagar
**Address:** 57 Tras St
Singapore 078996 Singapore
**Phone:** +65 6224 8186

#358
## Chit's Bar and Restaurant
**Cuisines:** Diners, Bar
**Average price:** $11-30
**District:** Changi
**Address:** 11 Changi Coast Walk
Singapore 499740 Singapore
**Phone:** +65 6214 9168

#359
## The Black Swan
**Cuisines:** Bars, Bistro
**Average price:** Above $61
**District:** Raffles Place
**Address:** 19 Cecil Street
Singapore 049704 Singapore
**Phone:** +65 8181 3305

#360
## Red Pig Korean BBQ
**Cuisines:** Korean
**Average price:** $11-30
**District:** Tanjong Pagar
**Address:** 93 Amoy Street
Singapore 069913 Singapore
**Phone:** +65 6220 7176

#361
## Botan Japanese Restaurant
**Cuisines:** Japanese
**Average price:** $11-30
**District:** Raffles Place
**Address:** 36 Pekin St
Singapore 048766 Singapore
**Phone:** +65 6536 4404

#362
## VeganBurg
**Cuisines:** Vegan, Burgers, Fast Food
**Average price:** $11-30
**District:** Bayfront
**Address:** 12 Marina Boulevard
Singapore 018982 Singapore
**Phone:** +65 6604 6018

#363
## Beng Hiang
**Cuisines:** Hokkien
**Average price:** $11-30
**District:** Bayfront
**Address:** 112 Amoy Street
Singapore 069932 Singapore
**Phone:** +65 6221 6684

#364
## Binomio
**Cuisines:** Spanish, Tapas
**Average price:** $11-30
**District:** Tanjong Pagar
**Address:** 20 Craig Road
Singapore 089692 Singapore
**Phone:** +65 6557 0547

#365
## Haramiya Japanese BBQ
**Cuisines:** Barbeque, Japanese
**Average price:** $11-30
**District:** Clarke Quay
**Address:** 6 Eu Tong Sen Street
Singapore 059817 Singapore
**Phone:** +65 6534 9468

#366
## Dimbulah
**Cuisines:** Cafe, Coffee & Tea
**Average price:** $11-30
**District:** Raffles Place
**Address:** 30 Raffles Place
Singapore 048622 Singapore
**Phone:** +65 6536 2949

#367
## Wharf Oyster Bar & Grill
**Cuisines:** Seafood, Bar
**Average price:** $31-60
**District:** Robertson Quay
**Address:** 60 Robertson Quay
Singapore 238252 Singapore
**Phone:** +65 6235 2466

#368
## Astons Specialties
**Average price:** $11-30
**District:** Bugis
**Address:** 201 Victoria Street
Singapore 188067 Singapore
**Phone:** +65 6884 5397

#369
## Beirut Grill
**Cuisines:** Halal, Vegetarian,
Middle Eastern
**Average price:** $11-30
**District:** Arab Street
**Address:** 72 Bussorah Street
Singapore 199485 Singapore
**Phone:** +65 6341 7728

#370
## Ichiban Boshi
**Cuisines:** Japanese, Sushi Bar
**Average price:** $11-30
**District:** River Valley
**Address:** 1 Kim Seng Promenade
Singapore 237994 Singapore
**Phone:** +65 6734 3433

#371
## Sakunthala's
**Cuisines:** Indian
**Average price:** $11-30
**District:** Little India
**Address:** 151 Dunlop St
Singapore 209466 Singapore
**Phone:** +65 6294 9159

#372
## The Soup Spoon
**Cuisines:** Soup
**Average price:** $11-30
**District:** Orchard
**Address:** 290 Orchard Road
Singapore 238859 Singapore
**Phone:** +65 6738 3860

#373
## Le Bistrot
**Cuisines:** French
**Average price:** Above $61
**District:** Kallang
**Address:** 2 Stadium Walk
Singapore 397691 Singapore
**Phone:** +65 6447 0018

#374
## Hong Kong Kim Gary Restaurant
**Average price:** $11-30
**District:** Harbourfront
**Address:** 1 Harbourfront Walk
Singapore 098585 Singapore
**Phone:** +65 6376 8183

#375
## Al-Azhar Eating
**Cuisines:** Halal
**Average price:** Under $10
**District:** Upper Bukit Timah
**Address:** 11/11a Cheong Chin Nam Rd
Singapore 599736 Singapore
**Phone:** +65 6466 5052

#376
## Tomi Sushi
**Cuisines:** Japanese
**Average price:** $11-30
**District:** Marine Parade, Katong
**Address:** 9 Raffles Boulevard Singapore
**Phone:** +65 6333 4633

#377
## E-Sarn Thai Corner
**Cuisines:** Thai
**Average price:** $11-30
**District:** Pasir Panjang
**Address:** 130 Pasir Panjang Road
Singapore 118548 Singapore
**Phone:** +65 6473 3716

#378
## The Missing Pan
**Cuisines:** Breakfast & Brunch,
Bakeries, Coffee & Tea
**Average price:** $11-30
**District:** Bukit Timah
**Address:** 619D Bukit Timah Road
Singapore 269724 Singapore
**Phone:** +65 6466 4377

#379
**Common Man Coffee Roasters**
**Cuisines:** Cafe
**Average price:** $31-60
**District:** Robertson Quay
**Address:** 22 Martin Road
Singapore 235098 Singapore
**Phone:** +65 6836 4695

#380
**Relish by Wild Rocket**
**Average price:** $11-30
**District:** Serangoon Gardens
**Address:** 1 Maju Avenue
Singapore 556679 Singapore
**Phone:** +65 6634 3422

#381
**Knead To Eat**
**Cuisines:** Coffee & Tea, Sandwiches
**Average price:** $11-30
**District:** Changi
**Address:** 6 Changi Business Park Ave 1
Singapore 486017 Singapore
**Phone:** +65 6702 0887

#382
**Melben Seafood**
**Cuisines:** Seafood
**Average price:** $31-60
**District:** Toa Payoh
**Address:** Blk 211 Lorong 8 Toa Payoh,
#01-11/15 Singapore 310211 Singapore
**Phone:** +65 6353 3120

#383
**Rakuzen Tampines**
**Cuisines:** Japanese
**Average price:** $31-60
**District:** Tampines
**Address:** 300 Tampines Avenue 5,
NTUC Income building
Singapore 529783 Singapore
**Phone:** +65 6786 8484

#384
**Karu's Indian Banana Leaf**
**Cuisines:** Indian
**Average price:** $11-30
**District:** Bukit Panjang
**Address:** 808/810 Upper Bukit Timah Rd
Singapore 678145 Singapore
**Phone:** +65 6762 7284

#385
**Soup Restaurant**
**Cuisines:** Chinese
**Average price:** $11-30
**District:** Boon Lay
**Address:** 1 Jurong West Central 2
Singapore 648886 Singapore
**Phone:** +65 6790 7797

#386
**Crystal Jade La Mian Xiao Long Bao**
**Cuisines:** Chinese
**Average price:** $11-30
**District:** Holland Village
**Address:** 241/241a Holland Ave
Singapore 278976 Singapore
**Phone:** +65 6463 0968

#387
**Everything WIth Fries**
**Cuisines:** Burgers
**Average price:** $11-30
**District:** Holland Village
**Address:** 40 Lorong Mambong
Singapore 277695 Singapore
**Phone:** +65 6463 3741

#388
**Arteastiq**
**Cuisines:** Bakeries, Desserts,
Coffee & Tea
**Average price:** $31-60
**District:** Somerset, Orchard
**Address:** 333 Orchard Road
Singapore 238867 Singapore
**Phone:** +65 6235 8370

#389
**My Little Spanish Place**
**Cuisines:** Spanish
**Average price:** $11-30
**District:** Bukit Timah
**Address:** 619 Bukit Timah Road
Singapore 269720 Singapore
**Phone:** +65 6463 2810

#390
**Coco Ichibanya**
**Cuisines:** Japanese
**Average price:** Under $10
**District:** Raffles Place
**Address:** 1 Vista Exchange Green
Singapore 138617 Singapore
**Phone:** +65 6570 2457

#391
**Original Sin**
**Cuisines:** Vegetarian
**Average price:** $31-60
**District:** Holland Village
**Address:** 43 Jln Merah Saga
Singapore 278115 Singapore
**Phone:** +65 6475 5605

#392
**Salads & Wraps**
**Cuisines:** Salad
**Average price:** $11-30
**District:** Tanjong Pagar
**Address:** Icon Village, 12 Gopeng St.
Singapore 078877 Singapore
**Phone:** +65 9433 3860

#393
**Oso Ristorante**
**Cuisines:** Italian
**Average price:** Above $61
**District:** Chinatown
**Address:** 46 Bukit Pasoh Rd
Singapore 089858 Singapore
**Phone:** +65 6222 9068

#394
**Tak Po**
**Cuisines:** Chinese
**Average price:** $11-30
**District:** Chinatown
**Address:** 42 Smith St
Singapore 058954 Singapore
**Phone:** +65 6225 0302

#395
**Señor Taco**
**Cuisines:** Mexican
**Average price:** $11-30
**District:** Bras Brasah
**Address:** #01-19/20 30 Victoria Street
Singapore 187996 Singapore
**Phone:** +65 6337 1377

#396
**B Bakery**
**Cuisines:**Bakeries, Desserts
**Average price:** $11-30
**District:** Arab Street
**Address:** 15 Bussorah Street
Singapore 199436 Singapore
**Phone:** +65 6293 9010

#397
**Happy Chef Western Foods**
**Average price:** $11-30
**District:** Lavender
**Address:** 465 Crawford Ln
Singapore 190465 Singapore
**Phone:** +65 6398 0773

#398
**Cedele**
**Cuisines:** Cafe
**Average price:** $11-30
**District:** Tanglin
**Address:** 501 Orchard Road #03-14
Singapore 238880 Singapore
**Phone:** +65 6732 8520

#399
**Fat Cow**
**Cuisines:** Japanese
**Average price:** $11-30
**District:** Tanglin
**Address:** 1 Orchard Blvd #01-01/02
Camden Medical Centre
Singapore 248649 Singapore
**Phone:** +65 6735 0308

#400
**Rk Eating House**
**Cuisines:** Indian
**Average price:** Under $10
**District:** Serangoon Gardens
**Address:** 1 Kensington Park Road
Singapore 557253 Singapore
**Phone:** +65 6289 5379

#401
**Bedrock Bar & Grill**
**Cuisines:** Bar
**Average price:** $11-30
**District:** Somerset, Orchard
**Address:** 01-05 Pan Pacific
Serviced Suites, 238163 Singapore
**Phone:** +65 6238 0054

#402
**Wooloomooloo Steakhouse**
**Cuisines:** Steakhouses
**Average price:** Above $61
**District:** Bras Brasah, City Hall
**Address:** 2 Stamford Road
Singapore 178882 Singapore
**Phone:** +65 6338 0261

#403
**Blackbird Cafe**
**Cuisines:** Desserts, Coffee & Tea
**Average price:** $11-30
**District:** Dhoby Ghaut, Mount Sophia
**Address:** 6 Handy Road, #01-01A,
The Luxe, 229234 Singapore
**Phone:** +65 6337 3448

#404
**Tawandang Microbrewery**
**Cuisines:** Bars, Thai, Beer,
Wine & Spirits
**Average price:** $31-60
**District:** Queenstown, Dempsey Hill
**Address:** 26 Dempsey Rd
Singapore 249686 Singapore
**Phone:** +65 6476 6742

#405
**Olive Tree Restaurant & Cafe**
**Cuisines:** Coffee & Tea, Buffets
**Average price:** Above $61
**District:** Bras Brasah
**Address:** 80 Middle Road
InterContinental Singapore
Singapore 188966 Singapore
**Phone:** +65 6431 1061

#406
**Medzs**
**Cuisines:** Mediterranean
**Average price:** $11-30
**District:** Somerset, Orchard
**Address:** 181 Orchard Road
Singapore 238896 Singapore
**Phone:** +65 6238 9028

#407
**Salad Stop!**
**Cuisines:** Salad
**Average price:** $11-30
**District:** Raffles Place
**Address:** 1 Raffles Place
Singapore 048616 Singapore
**Phone:** +65 6820 0160

#408
**Ya Kun Kaya Toast**
**Cuisines:** Coffee & Tea, Bakeries
**Average price:** $11-30
**District:** Raffles Place
**Address:** 18 China Street
Singapore 049560 Singapore
**Phone:** +65 6438 3638

#409
**Pizzeria L'Operetta**
**Cuisines:** Pizza, Italian
**Average price:** $11-30
**District:** Tanjong Pagar
**Address:** 12 Gopeng Street
Singapore 078877 Singapore
**Phone:** +65 6222 9487

#410
**Bacchanalia**
**Cuisines:** Modern European
**Average price:** Above $61
**District:** Dhoby Ghaut
**Address:** 23A Coleman Street
Singapore 179806 Singapore
**Phone:** +65 6509 1453

#411
**Mary's Kafe**
**Cuisines:** Cafe, Asian Fusion
**Average price:** Under $10
**District:** Bras Brasah
**Address:** 1 Queen St
Singapore 188534 Singapore
**Phone:** +65 6256 9696

#412
**The Pizza Place**
**Cuisines:** Pizza & Pasta
**Average price:** $11-30
**District:** Bras Brasah, City Hall
**Address:** 252 North Bridge Road,
Raffles City Shopping Centre, B1-16
Singapore 179103 Singapore
**Phone:** +65 6336 1979

#413
**Kiseki Japanese Buffet
Restaurant**
**Cuisines:** Japanese, Buffets
**Average price:** $31-60
**District:** Somerset, Orchard
**Address:** 181 Orchard Road
Singapore 238896 Singapore
**Phone:** +65 6736 1216

#414
**Tandoor Restaurant**
**Cuisines:** Indian
**Average price:** $31-60
**District:** Somerset, Orchard
**Address:** 11 Cavenagh Road
Singapore 229616 Singapore
**Phone:** +65 6730 0153

#415
**Sushi Ichi**
**Cuisines:** Japanese, Sushi Bar
**Average price:** Above $61
**District:** Orchard
**Address:** 6 Scotts Road
Singapore 228209 Singapore
**Phone:** +65 6299 0014

#416
**Whampoa Food Street Keng
Fish Head Steamboat Eating**
**Cuisines:** Seafood
**Average price:** $11-30
**District:** Novena
**Address:** 556 Balestier Road
Singapore 329872 Singapore
**Phone:** +65 9769 4451

#417
**Chilli Padi Nonya**
**Cuisines:** Chinese
**Average price:** $11-30
**District:** Joo Chiat
**Address:** 11 Joo Chiat Place
Singapore 427744 Singapore
**Phone:** +65 6275 1002

#418
**Ah Tai Chicken Rice**
**Cuisines:** Chinese
**Average price:** Under $10
**District:** Tanjong Pagar
**Address:** 1 Kadayanallur Street
Singapore 069184 Singapore
**Phone:** +65 8137 6559

#419
**Rokeby**
**Cuisines:** Bistro, Cafe, Bar
**Average price:** $11-30
**District:** Serangoon
**Address:** 15-9 Jalan Riang
Singapore 358972 Singapore
**Phone:** +65 9106 0437

#420
**Al-Ameen Makan House**
**Cuisines:** Indian
**Average price:** Under $10
**District:** Pasir Panjang
**Address:** 12 Clementi Road
Singapore 129742 Singapore
**Phone:** +65 6774 0637

#421
## Cha Cha Cha
**Cuisines:** Mexican
**Average price:** $11-30
**District:** Holland Village
**Address:** 32 Lorong Mambong
Singapore 277690 Singapore
**Phone:** +65 6462 1650

#422
## PoTeaTo
**Cuisines:** American
**Average price:** $11-30
**District:** Tiong Bahru
**Address:** 78 Yong Siak Street
Singapore 163078 Singapore
**Phone:** +65 6221 2488

#423
## Balzac Brasserie
**Cuisines:** Brasseries
**Average price:** Above $61
**District:** Bencoolen, Orchard
**Address:** 9 Bras Basah Road
Singapore 189559 Singapore
**Phone:** +65 6336 0797

#424
## Reddot Brewhouse
**Average price:** $11-30
**District:** Queenstown, Dempsey Hill
**Address:** 25a Dempsey Rd
Singapore 247691 Singapore
**Phone:** +65 6475 0500

#425
## Jewel Coffee
**Cuisines:** Coffee & Tea, Cafe
**Average price:** Under $10
**District:** Bayfront
**Address:** 1 Shenton Way
Singapore 068803 Singapore
**Phone:** +65 6636 9452

#426
## The Rotisserie
**Cuisines:** Salad, Burgers
**Average price:** Under $10
**District:** Raffles Place
**Address:** 51 Telok Ayer Street
Singapore 048441 Singapore
**Phone:** +65 6224 5486

#427
## Don Your Personal Pie Club
**Cuisines:** Cafe
**Average price:** $11-30
**District:** Raffles Place
**Address:** 20 Cross Street
Singapore 048422 Singapore
**Phone:** +65 6536 0925

#428
## Mouth Restaurant
**Cuisines:** Dim Sum, Cantonese
**Average price:** $11-30
**District:** Raffles Place
**Address:** 22 Cross Street
Singapore 048421 Singapore
**Phone:** +65 6438 5798

#429
## 136 Hong Kong Street
## Fish Head Steamboat
**Cuisines:** Chinese
**Average price:** Under $10
**District:** Ann Siang Hill, Tanjong Pagar
**Address:** 291 South Bridge Road
Singapore 058836 Singapore
**Phone:** +65 9437 8260

#430
## Trattoria Nonna Lina
**Cuisines:** Italian
**Average price:** $11-30
**District:** Duxton Hill, Tanjong Pagar
**Address:** 4 Craig Road
Singapore 089664 Singapore
**Phone:** +65 6222 0930

#431
## Enoteca L'Operetta
**Cuisines:** Italian
**Average price:** $11-30
**District:** Boat Quay
**Address:** 78-79 Boat Quay
Singapore 049867 Singapore
**Phone:** +65 6838 2482

#432
## Katanashi
**Cuisines:** Japanese
**Average price:** $11-30
**District:** Boat Quay
**Address:** 77 Boat Quay
Singapore 049865 Singapore
**Phone:** +65 6533 0490

#433
## Aussie Roll
**Cuisines:** Japanese, Sushi Bar
**Average price:** $11-30
**District:** Raffles Place
**Address:** 30 Raffles Place
Singapore 048622 Singapore
**Phone:** +65 6746 3077

#434
## Zheng Swee Kee
**Average price:** $11-30
**District:** Bras Brasah, City Hall
**Address:** 25 Seah Street
Singapore 188381 Singapore
**Phone:** +65 6338 3827

#435
**Ya Hua Bak Kut Teh**
**Cuisines:** Fast Food
**Average price:** $11-30
**District:** Tiong Bahru
**Address:** 593 Havelock Road
Singapore 169641 Singapore
**Phone:** +65 6222 9610

#436
**Cafe Brio's**
**Cuisines:** Cafe
**Average price:** $11-30
**District:** River Valley
**Address:** 392 Havelock Road
Singapore 169663 Singapore
**Phone:** +65 6233 1100

#437
**Shimbashi Soba**
**Average price:** $11-30
**District:** Orchard
**Address:** 290 Orch Rd
Singapore 238859 Singapore
**Phone:** +65 6735 9882

#438
**Open House**
**Cuisines:** Buffets
**Average price:** $31-60
**District:** Orchard
**Address:** 270 Orchard Road
Singapore 238857 Singapore
**Phone:** +65 6603 8855

#439
**The Moomba Tuckshop**
**Cuisines:** Sandwiches
**Average price:** $11-30
**District:** Bayfront
**Address:** 4 Battery Road #B1-01
Bank of China Building
Singapore 049908 Singapore
**Phone:** +65 6536 5235

#440
**Extra Virgin Pizza**
**Cuisines:** Pizza, Italian
**Average price:** $11-30
**District:** Newton, Novena
**Address:** United Square Shopping Mall,
101 Thomson Road
Singapore 307591 Singapore
**Phone:** +65 6247 5757

#441
**Waterfall Cafe**
**Cuisines:** Cafe
**Average price:** $11-30
**District:** Tanglin, Bukit Timah
**Address:** 22 Orange Grove Road
Singapore 258350 Singapore
**Phone:** +65 6213 4398

#442
**Assembly Coffee**
**Cuisines:** Cafe
**Average price:** $11-30
**District:** Bukit Timah
**Address:** 26 Evans Lodge
Singapore 259367 Singapore
**Phone:** +65 6735 5647

#443
**Trattoria L'Operetta**
**Cuisines:** Pizza, Italian
**Average price:** $31-60
**District:** Katong
**Address:** 244 Tanjong Katong Rd
Singapore 437032 Singapore
**Phone:** +65 6440 9322

#444
**Cedele**
**Cuisines:** Delis, Bakeries, Desserts
**Average price:** $11-30
**District:** Marine Parade
**Address:** 80 Marine Parade Road
Singapore 449269 Singapore
**Phone:** +65 6348 1535

#445
**Teochew Handmade Pau**
**Average price:** Under $10
**District:** Toa Payoh
**Address:** Blk 127 Toa Payoh Lor 1
Singapore 310127 Singapore
**Phone:** +65 6254 2053

#446
**Ichiban Boshi**
**Cuisines:** Japanese
**Average price:** $11-30
**District:** Marine Parade
**Address:** Marine Parade Road
Singapore 449269 Singapore
**Phone:** +65 6342 1013

#447
**Sin Hoi Sai Eating House**
**Cuisines:** Cafe, Coffee & Tea, Chinese
**Average price:** $11-30
**District:** Joo Chiat, Marine Parade
**Address:** 187 East Coast Rd
Singapore 428893 Singapore
**Phone:** +65 6440 6956

#448
**Seafood Paradise**
**Cuisines:** Chinese, Seafood
**Average price:** $11-30
**District:** Paya Lebar
**Address:** 91 Defu Lane 10
Singapore 539221 Singapore
**Phone:** +65 6487 2429

#449
**Poison Ivy**
**Cuisines:**
**Average price:** $11-30
**District:** Lim Chu Kang
**Address:** 100 Neo Tiew Road
Singapore 719026 Singapore
**Phone:** +65 6898 5001

#450
**Big Eater Seafood**
**Cuisines:** Chinese, Seafood
**Average price:** $31-60
**District:** Simei
**Address:** 34 Jln Pari Burong
Singapore 488700 Singapore
**Phone:** +65 6449 8066

#451
**Margarita's**
**Cuisines:** Mexican
**Average price:** Above $61
**District:** West Coast
**Address:** 108 Faber Drive
Singapore 129418 Singapore
**Phone:** +65 6777 1782

#452
**Spize - The Makan Place**
**Cuisines:** Halal
**Average price:** Under $10
**District:** Simei
**Address:** 336 Bedok Rd
Singapore 469512 Singapore
**Phone:** +65 6445 3211

#453
**Tuk Tuk**
**Cuisines:** Food, Thai
**Average price:** $11-30
**District:** Bayfront, Raffles Place
**Address:** Temasek Boulevard 3
Singapore 038983 Singapore
**Phone:** +65 6333 3362

#454
**Tapa King**
**Cuisines:** Street Vendors, Filipino
**Average price:** Under $10
**District:** Bayfront, Raffles Place
**Address:** 18 Raffles Quay
Singapore 048582 Singapore
**Phone:** +65 9187 2307

#455
**La Pizzaiola**
**Cuisines:** Pizza, Italian
**Average price:** $11-30
**District:** Tanjong Pagar
**Address:** 137 Telok Ayer Street
Singapore 068802 Singapore
**Phone:** +65 6222 0908

#456
**Ka-Soh**
**Cuisines:** Chinese
**Average price:** $11-30
**District:** Tanjong Pagar
**Address:** 96 Amoy St
Singapore 069916 Singapore
**Phone:** +65 6473 6686

#457
**Swee Kee Ka-Soh Fish-Head Noodle House**
**Cuisines:** Chinese
**Average price:** $11-30
**District:** Tanjong Pagar
**Address:** 96 Amoy Street
Singapore 069916 Singapore
**Phone:** +65 6224 9920

#458
**Hanoi Vietnamese Restaurant**
**Cuisines:** Vietnamese
**Average price:** $11-30
**District:** Tanjong Pagar
**Address:** 100 Tras Street
Singapore 079027 Singapore
**Phone:** +65 6444 4406

#459
**Canto Kitchen**
**Average price:** $11-30
**District:** Chinatown, Outram
**Address:** 1 Park Rd
Singapore 059108 Singapore
**Phone:** +65 6536 0501

#460
**Supply & Demand**
**Cuisines:** Italian
**Average price:** $11-30
**District:** Bayfront, City Hall
**Address:** 8 Raffles Ave
Singapore 039802 Singapore
**Phone:** +65 6336 0588

#461
**Bungy Bar**
**Cuisines:** Cafe, Pubs
**Average price:** $11-30
**District:** Clarke Quay
**Address:** 3E River Valley Road
Singapore 179024 Singapore
**Phone:** +65 6339 5707

#462
**The Corner Place Korean BBQ**
**Cuisines:** Korean
**Average price:** $11-30
**District:** City Hall
**Address:** 6 Raffles Boulevard
Singapore 039594 Singapore
**Phone:** +65 6333 0997

#463
## Table At 7
**Cuisines:** Indonesian, Australian
**Average price:** $11-30
**District:** Robertson Quay
**Address:** 7 Mohammed Sultan Road
Singapore 238957 Singapore
**Phone:** +65 6836 6362

#464
## Ting Heng Seafood Restaurant
**Cuisines:** Seafood
**Average price:** $11-30
**District:** Tiong Bahru
**Address:** Blk 82 Tiong Poh Road
Singapore 160082 Singapore
**Phone:** +65 6323 6093

#465
## Hua Ting Restaurant
**Cuisines:** Dim Sum
**Average price:** $31-60
**District:** Bencoolen, Orchard
**Address:** 442 Orchard Rd,
Level 2 Orchard Hotel
Singapore 189621 Singapore
**Phone:** +65 6739 6666

#466
## Crystal Jade Palace
**Average price:** $31-60
**District:** Orchard
**Address:** 391 Orch Rd
Singapore 238872 Singapore
**Phone:** +65 6735 2388

#467
## Jaggi's Northern Indian Cuisine
**Cuisines:** Indian
**Average price:** Under $10
**District:** Little India, Farrer Park
**Address:** 34-36 Race Crse Rd
Singapore 218553 Singapore
**Phone:** +65 6296 6141

#468
## Swaadhisht
**Cuisines:** Indian
**Average price:** $11-30
**District:** Little India
**Address:** 47 Chander Rd
Singapore 219546 Singapore
**Phone:** +65 6392 0513

#469
## Deli Turk Turkish Cuisine
**Cuisines:** Turkish
**Average price:** $11-30
**District:** Bayfront
**Address:** 03-004 Suntec City Mall
Singapore 038983 Singapore
**Phone:** +65 6336 8082

#470
## MTR 1924
**Cuisines:** Indian
**Average price:** Under $10
**District:** Little India
**Address:** 438 Serangoon Road
Singapore 218133 Singapore
**Phone:** +65 6296 5800

#471
## Buona Terra
**Cuisines:** Italian
**Average price:** Above $61
**District:** Newton
**Address:** 29 Scotts Road
Singapore 228224 Singapore
**Phone:** +65 6733 0209

#472
## McDonald's Kallang
**Cuisines:** Fast Food
**Average price:** $11-30
**District:** Kallang
**Address:** 200 Stadium Boulevard
Singapore 397726 Singapore
**Phone:** +65 6440 6010

#473
## Chihuly Lounge
**Cuisines:** Nightlife
**Average price:** $31-60
**District:** City Hall
**Address:** 7 Raffles Ave
Singapore 039799
Singapore
**Phone:** +65 6434 5288

#474
## The Audacious Cakery
**Cuisines:** Desserts, Bakeries
**Average price:** $31-60
**District:** Chinatown
**Address:** Blk 2 Everton Park, #01-61
Singapore 081002 Singapore
**Phone:** +65 6223 3047

#475
## The Olde Cuban
**Cuisines:** Tobacco Shops
**Average price:** $31-60
**District:** Chinatown
**Address:** 2 Trengganu Street
Singapore 058456 Singapore
**Phone:** +65 6222 2207

#476
## Wood Would
**Average price:** $31-60
**District:** Somerset, Orchard
**Address:** 333A Orchard Road
Singapore 238897 Singapore
**Phone:** +65 6735 6136

#477
## Chocolate Origin
**Cuisines:** Desserts
**Average price:** $11-30
**District:** Changi
**Address:** Block 4 Changi Village Road
Singapore 500004 Singapore
**Phone:** +65 6542 2939

#478
## Hong Kong Street Family Restaurant
**Cuisines:** Cantonese
**Average price:** $11-30
**District:** Newton, Novena
**Address:** 273 Thomson Road
Singapore 307644 Singapore
**Phone:** +65 6252 3132

#479
## Shinzo Japanese Cuisine
**Cuisines:** Japanese, Sushi Bar
**Average price:** Above $61
**District:** Clarke Quay
**Address:** 17 Carpenter Street
Singapore 059906 Singapore
**Phone:** +65 6438 2921

#480
## Sia Huat
**Average price:** $11-30
**District:** Chinatown
**Address:** 7 Temple Street
Singapore 058560 Singapore
**Phone:** +65 6223 1732

#481
## Qisahn
**Average price:** $11-30
**District:** Tanglin
**Address:** 545 Orchard Rd Far
East Shopping Centre
Singapore 238882 Singapore
**Phone:** +65 3110 3518

#482
## Poh Cheu
**Cuisines:** Food
**Average price:** Under $10
**District:** Alexandra
**Address:** 127 Bukit Merah Lane 1
Singapore 150127 Singapore
**Phone:** +65 6276 2287

#483
## St Andrew's Cathedral
**Average price:** $11-30
**District:** Bras Brasah, City Hall
**Address:** 11 Saint Andrew's Road
Singapore 178959 Singapore
**Phone:** +65 6337 6104

#484
## Durian Mpire by 717 Trading
**Cuisines:** Desserts, Bakeries
**Average price:** $31-60
**District:** Hougang
**Address:** 90 Hougang Avenue 10
Singapore 538766 Singapore
**Phone:** +65 6385 7717

#485
## Gong Cha
**Cuisines:** Coffee & Tea
**Average price:** Under $10
**District:** Novena
**Address:** 10 Sinaran Drive
Singapore 307506 Singapore
**Phone:** +65 6397 6816

#486
## Romankan Yokohama
**Cuisines:** Fast Food, Japanese
**Average price:** Under $10
**District:** Orchard
**Address:** Ngee Ann City, 391
Orchard Road, 238872 Singapore
**Phone:** +65 6738 2505

#487
## The Chocolate Bar
**Cuisines:** Desserts
**Average price:** $31-60
**District:** Bayfront
**Address:** 10 Bayfront Avenue
Singapore 018956
Singapore
**Phone:** +65 6688 8858

#488
## Sumo Salad
**Cuisines:** Health Markets
**Average price:** $31-60
**District:** Somerset, Orchard
**Address:** 313 Somerset Road
Singapore 238895 Singapore
**Phone:** +65 6238 9886

#489
## Open Door Policy
**Cuisines:** Cafe
**Average price:** Above $61
**District:** Tiong Bahru
**Address:** 19 Yong Siak St
Singapore 168650 Singapore
**Phone:** +65 6221 9307

#490
## LeVeL33
**Cuisines:** Bars, Gastropubs
**Average price:** $31-60
**District:** Bayfront
**Address:** 8 Marina Boulevard #33-01
Singapore 018981 Singapore
**Phone:** +65 6834 3133

#491
## Plaza Singapura
**Cuisines:** Shopping Centers
**Average price:** $11-30
**District:** Dhoby Ghaut, Mount Sophia
**Address:** 68 Orchard Road
Singapore 238839
Singapore
**Phone:** +65 6513 3585

#492
## Tanuki Raw
**Cuisines:** Japanese, Sushi Bar
**Average price:** $11-30
**District:** Somerset, Orchard
**Address:** 181 Orchard Road
Singapore 238896 Singapore
**Phone:** +65 6636 5949

#493
## Sim Lim Square
**Average price:** $11-30
**District:** Bencoolen
**Address:** 1 Rochor Canal Road
Singapore 188504 Singapore
**Phone:** +65 6338 3859

#494
## Peach Garden Noodle House
**Cuisines:** Dim Sum, Cantonese
**Average price:** $31-60
**District:** Changi
**Address:** 80 Airport Boulevard, Level 3
Singapore 819642 Singapore
**Phone:** +65 6546 7383

#495
## Tomato Express
**Cuisines:** American
**Average price:** $11-30
**District:** Dhoby Ghaut
**Address:** 68 Orchard Rd
Singapore 238839 Singapore
**Phone:** +65 6341 9162

#496
## Old Town White Coffee
**Cuisines:** Hainanese
**Average price:** Under $10
**District:** Novena
**Address:** 10 Sinaran Drive
Singapore 307506 Singapore
**Phone:** +65 6397 7078

#497
## Five Star Hainanese Chicken Rice
**Cuisines:** Coffee & Tea, Cafe,
Breakfast & Brunch
**Average price:** $11-30
**District:** Marine Parade, Katong
**Address:** 191 East Coast Rd
Singapore 428897 Singapore
**Phone:** +65 6777 5555

#498
## Platitos
**Cuisines:** Sandwiches
**Average price:** $31-60
**District:** Tanjong Pagar
**Address:** 1 Tras Link #01-08
Singapore 078867 Singapore
**Phone:** +65 6444 1654

#499
## Keystone Restaurant
**Cuisines:** European
**Average price:** Above $61
**District:** Tanjong Pagar
**Address:** 11 Stanley Street
Singapore 068730 Singapore
**Phone:** +65 6221 0046

#500
## Hot Star Large Fried Chicken
**Cuisines:** Chinese
**Average price:** Under $10
**District:** Little India
**Address:** 180 Kitchener Road
Singapore 208539 Singapore
**Phone:** +65 6634 8032

# TOP 200 BARS/PUBS

Recommended by Locals & Trevelers

(From #1 to #200)

#1
## 28 Hong Kong Street
Bar
**Average price:** Expensive
**District:** Clarke Quay
**Address:** 28 HongKong Street
Singapore 059667 Singapore
**Phone:** +65 6533 2001

#2
## Jigger and Pony
Cocktail Bar
**Average price:** Expensive
**District:** Tanjong Pagar
**Address:** 101 Amoy Street
Singapore 069921 Singapore
**Phone:** +65 6223 9101

#3
## Going Om
Bar, Cafe
**Average price:** Moderate
**District:** Arab Street
**Address:** 63 Haji Lane
Singapore 189256 Singapore
**Phone:** +65 6297 9197

#4
## Bar Stories
Bar
**Average price:** Expensive
**District:** Arab Street
**Address:** 55/57A Haji Lane
Singapore 189248 Singapore
**Phone:** +65 6298 0838

#5
## Bitters & Love
Champagne Bar
**Average price:** Moderate
**District:** Clarke Quay
**Address:** 36 North Canal Road
Singapore 059292 Singapore
**Phone:** +65 6438 1836

#6
## Ice Cold Beer
Bar
**Average price:** Moderate
**District:** Somerset, Orchard
**Address:** 9 Emerald Hill Road
Singapore 229293 Singapore
**Phone:** +65 6735 9929

#7
## City Space Swissôtel The Stamford
Wine Bar, Champagne Bar, Lounge
**Average price:** Exclusive
**District:** Bras Brasah, City Hall
**Address:** 2 Stamford Road
Singapore 178882 Singapore
**Phone:** +65 6837 3322

#8
## Wala Wala Cafe Bar
Bar
**Average price:** Moderate
**District:** Holland Village
**Address:** 31 Lorong Mambong
Singapore 277689 Singapore
**Phone:** +65 6462 4288

#9
## Cicheti
Wine Bar, Italian, Pizza
**Average price:** Moderate
**District:** Arab Street
**Address:** 52 Kandahar Street
Singapore 198901 Singapore
**Phone:** +65 6292 5012

#10
## No. 5
Bar
**Average price:** Moderate
**District:** Somerset, Orchard
**Address:** 5 Emerald Hill Road
Singapore 229289 Singapore
**Phone:** +65 6732 0818

#11
## 1-Altitude Gallery & Bar
Wine Bar, Lounge, Wineries
**Average price:** Expensive
**District:** Raffles Place
**Address:** 1 Raffles Place
Singapore 048616 Singapore
**Phone:** +65 6438 0410

#12
## Brewerkz
Bar
**Average price:** Expensive
**District:** Clarke Quay
**Address:** 30 Merchant Road
Singapore 058282 Singapore
**Phone:** +65 6438 7438

#13
## JiBiru Craft Beer Bar
Japanese, Bar
**Average price:** Moderate
**District:** Somerset, Orchard
**Address:** 313 Somerset
Singapore 238895 Singapore
**Phone:** +65 6732 6884

#14
## Long Bar
Wine Bar, Cocktail Bar
**Average price:** Exclusive
**District:** Bras Brasah, City Hall
**Address:** 1 Beach Road
Singapore 189673 Singapore
**Phone:** +65 6412 1816

#15
**OverEasy**
Bar, Diners, American
**Average price:** Moderate
**District:** Bayfront, Raffles Place
**Address:** 1 Fullerton Rd
Singapore 049213 Singapore
**Phone:** +65 6423 0701

#16
**Praelum Wine Bistro**
Wine Bar, Cafe
**Average price:** Expensive
**District:** Duxton Hill, Tanjong Pagar
**Address:** 4 Duxton Hill
Singapore 089590 Singapore
**Phone:** +65 6238 5287

#17
**Little Part 1**
Bar, American
**Average price:** Moderate
**District:** Thomson
**Address:** 15 Jasmine Road
Singapore 576584 Singapore
**Phone:** +65 6451 7553

#18
**2am: Dessert Bar**
Bar, Desserts, Coffee & Tea
**Average price:** Expensive
**District:** Holland Village
**Address:** 21a Lorong Liput
Singapore 277733 Singapore
**Phone:** +65 6291 9727

#19
**Orihara Shouten**
Bar, Japanese
**Average price:** Moderate
**District:** Robertson Quay
**Address:** 11 Unity St
Singapore 237995 Singapore
**Phone:** +65 6836 5710

#20
**Suprette**
Bar, American
**Average price:** Expensive
**District:** Little India
**Address:** 383 Jalan Besar
Singapore 209001 Singapore
**Phone:** +65 6298 8962

#21
**Coastes**
Bar
**Average price:** Moderate
**District:** Sentosa
**Address:** 50 Siloso Beach Walk
Singapore 099000 Singapore
**Phone:** +65 6274 9668

#22
**Satsuma Shochu Dining Bar**
Japanese, Bar
**Average price:** Moderate
**District:** Robertson Quay
**Address:** 1 Nanson Road,
#01-10/#02-10, 238909 Singapore
**Phone:** +65 6235 3565

#23
**Bedrock Bar & Grill**
Bar
**Average price:** Moderate
**District:** Somerset, Orchard
**Address:** 01-05 Pan Pacific Serviced
Suites
Singapore 238163 Singapore
**Phone:** +65 6238 0054

#24
**The Coastal Settlement**
Bar, Breakfast & Brunch
**Average price:** Expensive
**District:** Changi
**Address:** 200 Netheravon Road
Singapore 508529 Singapore
**Phone:** +65 6475 0200

#25
**Tanjong Beach Club**
Bar
**Average price:** Expensive
**District:** Sentosa
**Address:** 120 Tanjong Bch Walk
Singapore 098942 Singapore
**Phone:** +65 6270 1355

#26
**The Spiffy Dapper**
Cocktail Bar
**Average price:** Moderate
**District:** Boat Quay
**Address:** 2/F 61 Boat Quay
Singapore 049849 Singapore
**Phone:** +65 8233 9810

#27
**Standing Sushi Bar**
Japanese, Bar, Sushi Bar
**Average price:** Moderate
**District:** Bras Brasah
**Address:** 8 Queen Street
Singapore 188535 Singapore
**Phone:** +65 6333 1335

#28
**Mr Punch**
Pub, Food, Museum
**Average price:** Inexpensive
**District:** Bugis, Bras Brasah, City Hall
**Address:** 26 Seah Street
Singapore 188382 Singapore
**Phone:** +65 6334 5155

#29
**Paulaner Bräuhaus Singapore**
Bar, Cafe
**Average price:** Moderate
**District:** City Hall
**Address:** 9 Raffles Boulevard
Singapore 039596 Singapore
**Phone:** +65 6883 2572

#30
**KU DÉ TA**
Bar, Asian Fusion
**Average price:** Expensive
**District:** Bayfront
**Address:** 1 Bayfront Avenue Marina
Singapore 018971 Singapore
**Phone:** +65 6688 7688

#31
**Hood Bar and Cafe**
Bar, Cafe
**Average price:** Moderate
**District:** Bugis
**Address:** 201 Victoria Street
Singapore 188067 Singapore
**Phone:** +65 6221 8846

#32
**LeVeL33**
Bar, Gastropub
**Average price:** Expensive
**District:** Bayfront
**Address:** 8 Marina Boulevard #33-01
Singapore 018981 Singapore
**Phone:** +65 6834 3133

#33
**Tanuki Raw**
Japanese, Lounge, Sushi Bar
**Average price:** Moderate
**District:** Somerset, Orchard
**Address:** 181 Orchard Road
Singapore 238896 Singapore
**Phone:** +65 6636 5949

#34
**Nassim Hill**
Bar, Cafe, Bakeries
**Average price:** Moderate
**District:** Tanglin
**Address:** 56 Tanglin Road #01-03
Tanglin Post Office
Singapore 247964 Singapore
**Phone:** +65 6835 1128

#35
**Crazy Elephant**
Bar
**Average price:** Expensive
**District:** Clarke Quay
**Address:** 01-07 Clarke Quay
Singapore 179024 Singapore
**Phone:** +65 6337 1990

#36
**Sabio Tapas Bar**
Spanish, Bar
**Average price:** Exclusive
**District:** Duxton Hill, Tanjong Pagar
**Address:** 5 Duxton Hill
Singapore 089591 Singapore
**Phone:** +65 6690 7562

#37
**The White Rabbit**
Bar, European
**Average price:** Expensive
**District:** Queenstown
**Address:** 39C Harding Rd
Singapore 249541 Singapore
**Phone:** +65 9721 0536

#38
**Smith Street Taps**
Pub
**Average price:** Inexpensive
**District:** Chinatown
**Address:** Blk 335 Smith Street
Chinatown Complex
Singapore 050335 Singapore
**Phone:** +65 9430 2750

#39
**Cable Car 1890's Saloon Bar**
Bar
**Average price:** Moderate
**District:** Somerset, Orchard
**Address:** 49 Cuppage Road
Singapore 229466 Singapore
**Phone:** +65 6835 3545

#40
**Fern & Kiwi**
Sports Bar
**Average price:** Expensive
**District:** Clarke Quay
**Address:** 3C River Valley Rd
Singapore 179024 Singapore
**Phone:** +65 6336 2271

#41
**Garibaldi Italian
Restaurant & Bar**
Bar, Italian, European
**Average price:** Exclusive
**District:** Bugis, Bras Brasah, City Hall
**Address:** 36 Purvis Street
Singapore 188613 Singapore
**Phone:** +65 6837 1468

#42
**Fordham & Grand**
Bar
**Average price:** Moderate
**District:** Tanjong Pagar
**Address:** 43 Craig Road
Singapore 089681 Singapore
**Phone:** +65 6221 3088

#43
## Boomarang Bistro & Bar
Bar, Breakfast & Brunch
**Average price:** Moderate
**District:** Robertson Quay
**Address:** 01-15 The Quayside
Singapore 238252 Singapore
**Phone:** +65 6738 1077

#44
## Tantric
Gay Bar
**Average price:** Moderate
**District:** Chinatown
**Address:** 78 Neil Road
Singapore 088841 Singapore
**Phone:** +65 9245 8556

#45
## Wine Connection Bar & Bistro
Wine Bar
**Average price:** Moderate
**District:** Somerset, Orchard
**Address:** 41 Cuppage Road
Singapore 229462 Singapore
**Phone:** +65 6836 9069

#46
## Fandango Tapas & Wine Bar
Bar, Tapas/Small Plates
**Average price:** Exclusive
**District:** Bras Brasah
**Address:** 30 Victoria Street
Singapore 187996 Singapore
**Phone:** +65 6333 3450

#47
## Lot, Stock & Barrel Pub
Pub
**Average price:** Inexpensive
**District:** Bras Brasah, City Hall
**Address:** 30 Seah Street
Singapore 188386 Singapore
**Phone:** +65 6338 5540

#48
## Muddy Murphy's
Pub, Irish
**Average price:** Moderate
**District:** Tanglin
**Address:** 111 Somerset Road
Singapore 238879 Singapore
**Phone:** +65 6735 0400

#49
## The Halia At Raffles Hotel
Cocktail Bar, Asian Fusion
**Average price:** Expensive
**District:** Bras Brasah, City Hall
**Address:** 1 Beach Road
Singapore 189673 Singapore
**Phone:** +65 9639 1148

#50
## Fatboy's The Burger Bar
Bar, Burgers
**Average price:** Moderate
**District:** Thomson
**Address:** 187 Upper Thomson Rd
Singapore 574335 Singapore
**Phone:** +65 6252 8780

#51
## Hombre Cantina
Mexican, Bar
**Average price:** Moderate
**District:** Boat Quay
**Address:** 53 Boat Quay
Singapore 049842 Singapore
**Phone:** +65 6438 6708

#52
## The Black Swan
Bar, Bistro
**Average price:** Exclusive
**District:** Raffles Place
**Address:** 19 Cecil Street
Singapore 049704 Singapore
**Phone:** +65 8181 3305

#53
## The Cider Pit
Pub
**Average price:** Inexpensive
**District:** Joo Chiat
**Address:** 328 Joo Chiat Road
Singapore 427585 Singapore
**Phone:** +65 6440 0504

#54
## Brussels Sprouts
Pub, Belgian
**Average price:** Moderate
**District:** Robertson Quay
**Address:** 80 Mohamed Sultan Road
Singapore 239013 Singapore
**Phone:** +65 6887 4344

#55
## Colbar - Colonial Bar
Bar, Local Flavor
**Average price:** Expensive
**District:** Wessex Estate
**Address:** 9A Whitchurch Rd
Singapore 138839 Singapore
**Phone:** +65 6779 4859

#56
## Bar Bar Black Sheep
Bar, Cafe
**Average price:** Inexpensive
**District:** Sixth Avenue, Bukit Timah
**Address:** 879 Cherry Avenue
Singapore 279892 Singapore
**Phone:** +65 6468 9382

#57
**Tawandang Microbrewery**
Bar, Thai, Beer, Wine & Spirits
**Average price:** Expensive
**District:** Queenstown, Dempsey Hill
**Address:** 26 Dempsey Rd
Singapore 249686 Singapore
**Phone:** +65 6476 6742

#58
**Nektar**
Bar
**Average price:** Moderate
**District:** Newton
**Address:** 31 Scotts Road
Singapore 228225 Singapore
**Phone:** +65 6836 9185

#59
**Brewerkz**
Bar
**Average price:** Moderate
**District:** Kallang
**Address:** 2 Stadium Walk
Singapore 397691 Singapore
**Phone:** +65 6345 9905

#60
**Cuscaden Patio Cafe & Pub**
Pub
**Average price:** Moderate
**District:** Tanglin
**Address:** 21 Cuscaden Road
Singapore 249720 Singapore
**Phone:** +65 6887 3319

#61
**DARTSSoul Cafe & Bar**
Bar
**Average price:** Moderate
**District:** Bugis
**Address:** 201 Victoria Street
Singapore 188067 Singapore
**Phone:** +65 6636 9951

#62
**Caveau**
Wine Bar
**Average price:** Moderate
**District:** Tanglin
**Address:** Shaw Centre 1 Scotts Rd
Singapore 358666 Singapore
**Phone:** +65 6737 2622

#63
**Handlebar**
Bar
**Average price:** Moderate
**District:** Sembawang
**Address:** 57 Jalan Mempurong
Singapore 759057 Singapore
**Phone:** +65 6475 9571

#64
**Stärker Fresh Beer**
Bar
**Average price:** Moderate
**District:** Holland Village
**Address:** 25 Lorong Mambong
Singapore 277684 Singapore
**Phone:** +65 6465 8368

#65
**Cuscaden @ CHIJMES**
Bar
**Average price:** Moderate
**District:** Bras Brasah
**Address:** 30 Victoria Street #01-04
Singapore 187996 Singapore
**Phone:** +65 6338 3510

#66
**Wine Connection**
Wine Bar, Beer, Wine & Spirits
**Average price:** Moderate
**District:** Marine Parade, Katong
**Address:** 112 East Coast Rd
Singapore 428802 Singapore
**Phone:** +65 6346 6588

#67
**Piedra Negra**
Mexican, Bar
**Average price:** Moderate
**District:** Arab Street
**Address:** 241 Beach Road
Singapore 189753 Singapore
**Phone:** +65 6291 1297

#68
**Beer Market**
Bar
**Average price:** Expensive
**District:** Clarke Quay
**Address:** 3B River Valley Road
Singapore 179021 Singapore
**Phone:** +65 9661 8283

#69
**Attica**
Bar
**Average price:** Moderate
**District:** Clarke Quay
**Address:** 3A River Valley Rd
Singapore 179020 Singapore
**Phone:** +65 6333 9973

#70
**Immigrants**
Bar
**Average price:** Expensive
**District:** Joo Chiat
**Address:** 467 Joo Chiat Road
Singapore 427678 Singapore
**Phone:** +65 8511 7322

#71
**The New Harbour Cafe & Bar**
Bar, Cafe
**Average price:** Moderate
**District:** Duxton Hill, Tanjong Pagar
**Address:** 114 Tanjong Pagar Road
Singapore 088529 Singapore
**Phone:** +65 6226 2657

#72
**Harry's**
Bar
**Average price:** Moderate
**District:** Bayfront, City Hall
**Address:** 8 Raffles Ave
Singapore 039802 Singapore
**Phone:** +65 6334 0132

#73
**China One**
Bar, Dance Club
**Average price:** Moderate
**District:** Lavender
**Address:** Block 3E River Valley Road
Singapore 179024 Singapore
**Phone:** +65 6339 0280

#74
**Sidewalk Tavern**
Pub
**Average price:** Moderate
**District:** Siglap
**Address:** 924 East Coast Rd
Singapore 459115 Singapore
**Phone:** +65 6448 5979

#75
**Barkode Cocktail Bar**
Bar
**Average price:** Moderate
**District:** Little India
**Address:** 66 Dunlop St
Singapore 209394 Singapore
**Phone:** +65 6396 4463

#76
**Eight**
European, Wine Bar, Asian
**Average price:** Exclusive
**District:** Chinatown
**Address:** 8 Bukit Pasoh Road
Singapore 089822 Singapore
**Phone:** +65 6220 4513

#77
**Keyaki**
Bar, Japanese
**Average price:** Moderate
**District:** City Hall
**Address:** 7 Raffles Blvd
Singapore 039595 Singapore
**Phone:** +65 6826 8240

#78
**Wabar**
Bar
**Average price:** Moderate
**District:** Duxton Hill, Tanjong Pagar
**Address:** 62 Tanjong Pagar Road
Singapore 088483 Singapore
**Phone:** +65 6224 7073

#79
**The Old Brown Shoe**
Pub
**Average price:** Moderate
**District:** Bukit Timah
**Address:** 619f Bukit Timah Road
Singapore 269726 Singapore
**Phone:** +65 6468 4626

#80
**5 Izakaya Bar**
Bar
**Average price:** Moderate
**District:** Bayfront, Raffles Place
**Address:** 16 Collyer Quay
Singapore 049318 Singapore
**Phone:** +65 6536 8955

#81
**The Vault**
Bar, Music Venue
**Average price:** Exclusive
**District:** Boat Quay
**Address:** 23 Circular Road
Singapore 049379 Singapore
**Phone:** +65 6223 9695

#82
**Owls Brew**
Pub, Gastropub
**Average price:** Moderate
**District:** Mount Sophia
**Address:** 146 MacKenzie Road
Singapore 228723 Singapore
**Phone:** +65 6333 3440

#83
**Little Saigon**
Vietnamese, Pub, Ethnic Food
**Average price:** Exclusive
**District:** Clarke Quay
**Address:** Blk E River Valley Road
Singapore 179024 Singapore
**Phone:** +65 6337 5585

#84
**Fuse**
Bar, Cafe
**Average price:** Expensive
**District:** Bayfront
**Address:** 8 Bayfront Avenue
Singapore 018955 Singapore
**Phone:** +65 6688 5529

#85
## Owl Bar
Bar
**Average price:** Moderate
**District:** Outram
**Address:** 2 College Road
Singapore 169850 Singapore
**Phone:** +65 9299 6898

#86
## OChre
Bar, Italian
**Average price:** Expensive
**District:** Somerset, Orchard
**Address:** 181 Orchard Rd
Singapore 238896 Singapore
**Phone:** +65 6634 0423

#87
## Loof
Bar
**Average price:** Moderate
**District:** Bugis, Bras Brasah
**Address:** 03-07 Odeon Towers
Ext Rooftop, 188720 Singapore
**Phone:** +65 6338 8035

#88
## K Suites
Bar, Karaoke
**Average price:** Moderate
**District:** Bugis
**Address:** 201 Victoria Street
Singapore 188067 Singapore
**Phone:** +65 6243 3113

#89
## Ambrosia
Pub
**Average price:** Moderate
**District:** Arab Street
**Address:** 19 Baghdad St
Singapore 199658 Singapore
**Phone:** +65 6292 7313

#90
## The Tippling Club
Bar
**Average price:** Moderate
**District:** Duxton Hill, Tanjong Pagar
**Address:** 38 Tanjong Pagar Road
Singapore 088461 Singapore
**Phone:** +65 6475 2217

#91
## DYMK
Gay Bar
**Average price:** Moderate
**District:** Duxton Hill, Tanjong Pagar
**Address:** 41 Neil Road
Singapore 088824 Singapore
**Phone:** +65 6224 3965

#92
## The Handlebar
American, Bar
**Average price:** Moderate
**District:** Bayfront, Raffles Place
**Address:** Lock Road 01-01 Singapore
**Phone:** +65 6475 9571

#93
## Wine Connection @ Anchorpoint
Wine Bar
**Average price:** Moderate
**District:** Queenstown, Alexandra
**Address:** 370 Alexandra Road, #B1-08
Singapore 159953 Singapore
**Phone:** +65 6476 8997

#94
## Charlie's Tapas Grill & Bar
Sports Bar, Spanish
**Average price:** Moderate
**District:** Raffles Place, Boat Quay
**Address:** 32 Boat Quay
Singapore 049821 Singapore
**Phone:** +65 6533 5880

#95
## The Wine Company
Wine Bar
**Average price:** Moderate
**District:** Sentosa
**Address:** 6 Sentosa Gateway
Singapore 098072 Singapore
**Phone:** +65 6376 9029

#96
## KPO Cafe Bar
Bar
**Average price:** Moderate
**District:** Somerset, Orchard
**Address:** 1 Killiney Rd
Singapore 239518 Singapore
**Phone:** +65 6733 3648

#97
## Highlander Bar
Bar
**Average price:** Moderate
**District:** Clarke Quay
**Address:** 3B River Valley Road
Singapore 179021 Singapore
**Phone:** +65 6235 9528

#98
## Park
Pub, Bistro, Delicatessen
**Average price:** Moderate
**District:** Holland Village
**Address:** 281 Holland Avenue
Singapore 278621 Singapore
**Phone:** +65 9183 4224

#99
**The Pit Restaurant & Bar**
Bar, Restaurant
**Average price:** Moderate
**District:** Holland Village
**Address:** 21 Lorong Liput Holland Vlg
Singapore 277736 Singapore
**Phone:** +65 6468 3468

#100
**Drink Culture**
Beer, Wine & Spirits, Lounge
**Average price:** Moderate
**District:** Chinatown
**Address:** 51 Kreta Ayer Rd
Singapore 089008 Singapore
**Phone:** +65 6557 0538

#101
**Esmirada**
Bar
**Average price:** Expensive
**District:** Tanglin
**Address:** 442 Orch Rd
Singapore 238879 Singapore
**Phone:** +65 6735 3476

#102
**Halo Rooftop Lounge**
Bar
**Average price:** Moderate
**District:** Lavender
**Address:** 231 Outram Road
Singapore 169040 Singapore
**Phone:** +65 6595 1380

#103
**Prelude Rooftop Bar**
Bar
**Average price:** Moderate
**District:** Bayfront, Raffles Place
**Address:** 3 Fullerton Rd #04-01
Singapore 049215 Singapore
**Phone:** +65 6538 9038

#104
**i Darts Senso Bar**
Pub
**Average price:** Expensive
**District:** Robertson Quay
**Address:** 27 Mohamed Sultan Road
Singapore 238971 Singapore
**Phone:** +65 6737 3162

#105
**Lobby Court**
Bar
**Average price:** Moderate
**District:** Tanglin
**Address:** 22 Orange Grv Rd
Singapore 258350 Singapore
**Phone:** +65 6431 6156

#106
**Celina's GastroBar**
Bar
**Average price:** Moderate
**District:** Duxton Hill, Tanjong Pagar
**Address:** 51 Duxton Road
Singapore 089515 Singapore
**Phone:** +65 6220 1684

#107
**OKB**
Wine Bar, Bakeries
**Average price:** Moderate
**District:** Chinatown
**Address:** 1 Kampong Bahru Road
Singapore 169339 Singapore
**Phone:** +65 6220 4711

#108
**Porterhouse - Grill & Bar**
Bar, American
**Average price:** Moderate
**District:** Somerset
**Address:** 113 Killiney Road
Singapore 239550 Singapore
**Phone:** +65 6732 5113

#109
**Taboo Cafe & Bar**
Bar, Dance Club
**Average price:** Moderate
**District:** Tanjong Pagar, Chinatown
**Address:** 65 Neil Road
Singapore 088897 Singapore
**Phone:** +65 6225 6256

#110
**Balaclava**
Pub, Music Venue
**Average price:** Expensive
**District:** Orchard
**Address:** 2 Orchard Turn
Singapore 238801 Singapore
**Phone:** +65 6339 1600

#111
**Zushi Bar**
Bar
**Average price:** Inexpensive
**District:** Serangoon
**Address:** 301 Serangoon Avenue 2
Singapore 550301 Singapore
**Phone:** +65 6858 4929

#112
**Obama's Irish Pub**
Bar
**Average price:** Moderate
**District:** Tanjong Pagar
**Address:** 54 Tras Street Tanjong Pagar
Singapore 078993 Singapore
**Phone:** +65 6225 1090

#113
**Jekyll & Hyde**
Cocktail Bar
**Average price:** Moderate
**District:** Tanjong Pagar
**Address:** 49 Tras Street
Singapore 078988 Singapore
**Phone:** +65 6222 3349

#114
**Manhattan**
Cocktail Bar
**Average price:** Moderate
**District:** Tanglin
**Address:** 1 Cuscaden Road
Singapore 249715 Singapore
**Phone:** +65 6725 3377

#115
**Bikini Bar**
Bar
**Average price:** Moderate
**District:** Sentosa
**Address:** 50 Siloso Beach Walk
Singapore 099000 Singapore
**Phone:** +65 6276 6070

#116
**Quaruba'r**
Bar
**Average price:** Moderate
**District:** Siglap
**Address:** 113 Frankel Avenue
Singapore 458230 Singapore
**Phone:** +65 6243 0113

#117
**Play**
Bar, Dance Club
**Average price:** Moderate
**District:** Duxton Hill, Tanjong Pagar
**Address:** 21 Tanjong Pagar Rd
Singapore 088444 Singapore
**Phone:** +65 6227 7400

#118
**Dallas Restaurant & Bar**
American, Bar
**Average price:** Moderate
**District:** Raffles Place, Boat Quay
**Address:** 31 Boat Quay
Singapore 049820 Singapore
**Phone:** +65 6532 2131

#119
**Alley Bar**
Bar, Restaurant
**Average price:** Moderate
**District:** Somerset, Orchard
**Address:** 180 Orchard Road
Singapore 238846 Singapore
**Phone:** +65 6738 8818

#120
**Lucky 13**
Bar, Latin American
**Average price:** Expensive
**District:** Somerset, Orchard
**Address:** 111 Somerset Road #01-02
TripleOne Somerset
Singapore 238164 Singapore
**Phone:** +65 6733 9800

#121
**Brotzeit German Bier Bar**
Bar, German
**Average price:** Moderate
**District:** Somerset, Orchard
**Address:** 313 Orchard Road
Singapore 238895 Singapore
**Phone:** +65 6834 4038

#122
**Kazbar**
Bar
**Average price:** Expensive
**District:** Raffles Place
**Address:** 01-03 Capital Sq
Singapore 049482 Singapore
**Phone:** +65 6438 2975

#123
**Wiser Karaoke Lounge & Pub**
Pub, Karaoke
**Average price:** Inexpensive
**District:** Jurong
**Address:** 11 Japanese Garden Road
Singapore 619229 Singapore
**Phone:** +65 6261 1211

#124
**Orgo Bar and Restaurant**
Bar
**Average price:** Moderate
**District:** Bayfront, City Hall
**Address:** #04-01. Roof Terrace
Singapore 039802 Singapore
**Phone:** +65 9733 6911

#125
**Hosted On The Patio**
Mediterranean, Bar
**Average price:** Moderate
**District:** Alexandra
**Address:** 991B Alexandra Road
Singapore 119970 Singapore
**Phone:** +65 6276 7337

#126
**Bar Bar Black Sheep**
Bar
**Average price:** Moderate
**District:** Katong
**Address:** 363 Tanjong Katong Road
Singapore 437121 Singapore
**Phone:** +65 6348 8275

#127
**The Dubliner Irish Pub**
Pub, Art & Entertainment
**Average price:** Moderate
**District:** Somerset, Orchard
**Address:** 165 Penang Rd
Singapore 238461 Singapore
**Phone:** +65 6735 2220

#128
**Quaich Bar at Grand Copthorne Waterfront**
Bar
**Average price:** Moderate
**District:** River Valley
**Address:** 390A Havelock Road
Singapore 169664 Singapore
**Phone:** +65 6732 3452

#129
**Sara's at Upper Thompson**
Pub
**Average price:** Moderate
**District:** Thomson
**Address:** 217 Upper Thomson Road
Singapore 574350 Singapore
**Phone:** +65 6457 9868

#130
**Vida Vino**
Wine Bar
**Average price:** Expensive
**District:** Chinatown
**Address:** 29 Keong Saik Road
Singapore 089136 Singapore
**Phone:** +65 6222 1963

#131
**Pind Balluchi Bar & Grill**
Indian, Cocktail Bar, Lounge
**Average price:** Moderate
**District:** Clarke Quay
**Address:** 3B River Valley Road
Singapore 179021 Singapore
**Phone:** +65 6337 7350

#132
**Night & Day**
Bar
**Average price:** Moderate
**District:** Mount Sophia
**Address:** 139 A/c Selegie Rd
Singapore 188309 Singapore
**Phone:** +65 6884 5523

#133
**Señor Santos**
Bar
**Average price:** Moderate
**District:** Clarke Quay
**Address:** 01-12 Clarke Quay
Singapore 179021 Singapore
**Phone:** +65 6336 7741

#134
**Backstage Bar**
Bar
**Average price:** Inexpensive
**District:** Chinatown
**Address:** 13a Trengganu St
Singapore 058467 Singapore
**Phone:** +65 6392 3913

#135
**&SONS**
Wine Bar, Italian, Bistro
**Average price:** Moderate
**District:** Raffles Place
**Address:** 20 Cross Street, #01-19
Singapore 048422 Singapore
**Phone:** +65 6221 3937

#136
**BRIX**
Bar
**Average price:** Expensive
**District:** Orchard
**Address:** 10-12 Scotts Road
Singapore 228211 Singapore
**Phone:** +65 6732 1234

#137
**Moosehead Kitchen Bar**
Bar, Tapas/Small Plates
**Average price:** Moderate
**District:** Raffles Place
**Address:** 110 Telok Ayer Street
Singapore 068579 Singapore
**Phone:** +65 6636 8055

#138
**Vie Bar**
Pub
**Average price:** Moderate
**District:** Siglap
**Address:** 914 East Coast Rd
Singapore 459108 Singapore
**Phone:** +65 6245 0010

#139
**L'Aiglon**
Cocktail Bar
**Average price:** Expensive
**District:** Tanjong Pagar, Chinatown
**Address:** 69 Neil Rd
Singapore 088899 Singapore
**Phone:** +65 6220 0369

#140
**Insomnia**
Bar
**Average price:** Moderate
**District:** Bras Brasah
**Address:** 01-21 Chijmes
Singapore 187996 Singapore
**Phone:** +65 6338 6883

#141
**Uncabunca**
Pub
**Average price:** Moderate
**District:** Robertson Quay
**Address:** 80 Mohamed Sultan Road
Singapore 239013 Singapore
**Phone:** +65 6735 9848

#142
**Speakeasy**
Bar
**Average price:** Moderate
**District:** Duxton Hill, Tanjong Pagar
**Address:** 50 Tanjong Pagar Road
Singapore 088471 Singapore
**Phone:** +65 9644 9825

#143
**Alegro**
Bar, Spanish
**Average price:** Moderate
**District:** Clarke Quay
**Address:** 01-13 Clarke Quay
Singapore 179023 Singapore
**Phone:** +65 6883 0620

#144
**Bar Bar Black Sheep**
Bar
**Average price:** Moderate
**District:** Robertson Quay
**Address:** 01-04 Robertson Blue
Singapore 238245 Singapore
**Phone:** +65 2009 0511

#145
**Le Noir**
Bar
**Average price:** Moderate
**District:** Clarke Quay
**Address:** 3C River Valley Road
Singapore 179022 Singapore
**Phone:** +65 6339 6365

#146
**Ying Yang Rooftop Bar**
Bar
**Average price:** Moderate
**District:** Ann Siang Hill, Tanjong Pagar
**Address:** The Club, 28 Ann Siang Rd
Singapore 069708 Singapore
**Phone:** +65 6808 2188

#147
**Bull & Bear**
Bar
**Average price:** Moderate
**District:** Raffles Place
**Address:** 31 Pekin Street
Singapore 048671 Singapore
**Phone:** +65 6557 0879

#148
**District 10 Bar & Restaurant**
Bar, Bistro, Coffee & Tea
**Average price:** Expensive
**District:** Robertson Quay
**Address:** 81 Clemenceau Ave
Singapore 239917 Singapore
**Phone:** +65 6738 4788

#149
**Bartini**
Bar
**Average price:** Moderate
**District:** Ann Siang Hill, Tanjong Pagar
**Address:** 46 Club Street
Singapore 069423 Singapore
**Phone:** +65 6221 1025

#150
**Acid Bar**
Bar, Music Venue
**Average price:** Moderate
**District:** Somerset, Orchard
**Address:** 180 Orchard Rd
Singapore 238846 Singapore
**Phone:** +65 6738 8828

#151
**Aquanova**
Bar, Music Venue
**Average price:** Moderate
**District:** Clarke Quay
**Address:** 3 River Valley Rd
Singapore 179022 Singapore
**Phone:** +65 6305 6733

#152
**Brauhaus**
German, Pub
**Average price:** Moderate
**District:** Newton, Novena
**Address:** 101 Thomson Rd
Singapore 307591 Singapore
**Phone:** +65 6250 3116

#153
**Octapas Spanish Tapas Bar**
Spanish, Bar, Music Venue
**Average price:** Expensive
**District:** Clarke Quay
**Address:** River Valley Road
Singapore 179023 Singapore
**Phone:** +65 6837 2938

#154
**Mel's Place**
Bar
**Average price:** Expensive
**District:** Marine Parade, Katong
**Address:** 2A Kuo Chuan Avenue
Singapore 426897 Singapore
**Phone:** +65 6440 3573

#155
**Olivia Cassivelaun Fancourt**
Cocktail Bar, Lounge, French
**Average price:** Moderate
**District:** City Hall
**Address:** 1 Old Parliament Lane #02-02
Singapore 179429 Singapore
**Phone:** +65 6333 9312

#156
**Actors The Jam Bar**
Pub
**Average price:** Moderate
**District:** Boat Quay, Clarke Quay
**Address:** 13a South Bridge Rd
Singapore 058657 Singapore
**Phone:** +65 6535 3270

#157
**St. James Power Station**
Bar, Cafe, Coffee & Tea
**Average price:** Moderate
**District:** Harbourfront
**Address:** 3 Sentosa Gtwy
Singapore 098544 Singapore
**Phone:** +65 6270 7676

#158
**Forest Darts Cafe & Pub**
Pub, Karaoke
**Average price:** Moderate
**District:** Ann Siang Hill, Tanjong Pagar
**Address:** 45 Ann Siang Road
Singapore 069719 Singapore
**Phone:** +65 6227 3522

#159
**Hanamco**
Pub
**Average price:** Moderate
**District:** Changi
**Address:** Changi Village Rd 5
Singapore 500005 Singapore
**Phone:** +65 6543 1754

#160
**Pub Starlet**
Pub
**Average price:** Moderate
**District:** Thomson
**Address:** No.20 Jalan Leban
Singapore 577556 Singapore
**Phone:** +65 6553 0425

#161
**Cow & Coolies Karaoke Pub**
Bar, Karaoke
**Average price:** Moderate
**District:** Chinatown
**Address:** 30 Mosque Street
Singapore 059508 Singapore
**Phone:** +65 6221 1239

#162
**Black & White**
**Cocktail Bar & Bites**
Bar
**Average price:** Moderate
**District:** Robertson Quay
**Address:** 11 Unity Street
Singapore 237995 Singapore
**Phone:** +65 6836 5752

#163
**Koi Sushi and Izakaya**
Japanese, Pub
**Average price:** Moderate
**District:** Ann Siang Hill, Tanjong Pagar
**Address:** 89 Club St.
Singapore 069457 Singapore
**Phone:** +65 6225 5915

#164
**TBB Tiong Bahru Bar**
Wine Bar, Gastropub, Music Venue
**Average price:** Moderate
**District:** Tiong Bahru
**Address:** 3 Seng Poh Road
Singapore 168891 Singapore
**Phone:** +65 6438 4380

#165
**Oosters**
Bar, Belgian
**Average price:** Expensive
**District:** Raffles Place
**Address:** 25 Church St
Singapore 049482 Singapore
**Phone:** +65 6438 3210

#166
**Habitat**
Bar
**Average price:** Moderate
**District:** Robertson Quay
**Address:** 11 Unity Street #01-10/11
Robertson Walk
Singapore 237995 Singapore
**Phone:** +65 6732 6098

#167
**The Vintage Room**
Bar
**Average price:** Moderate
**District:** Duxton Hill, Tanjong Pagar
**Address:** 37 Duxton Hill
Singapore 089615 Singapore
**Phone:** +65 6690 7565

#168
**Harry's**
Bar
**Average price:** Moderate
**District:** Queenstown, Dempsey Hill
**Address:** Blk 11 Dempsey Road
Singapore 249673 Singapore
**Phone:** +65 6471 9018

#169
**Flying Hog Cafe & Bar**
Bar, Cafe
**Average price:** Moderate
**District:** Duxton Hill, Tanjong Pagar
**Address:** 32A Duxton Rd
Singapore 089496 Singapore
**Phone:** +65 6327 1518

#170
**Beach Cabana**
Bar
**Average price:** Moderate
**District:** Marine Parade
**Address:** 1000 East Coast Pkwy
Singapore 449876 Singapore
**Phone:** +65 6344 4773

#171
**Molly Roffey's Irish Pub**
Pub, Irish, American
**Average price:** Moderate
**District:** City Hall
**Address:** 8 Raffles Avenue
Singapore 039802 Singapore
**Phone:** +65 6238 1875

#172
**Magic Carpet**
Hookah Bar
**Average price:** Moderate
**District:** Arab Street
**Address:** 72 Bussorah Street
Singapore 199485 Singapore
**Phone:** +65 6341 7728

#173
**The Green Door**
Bar
**Average price:** Moderate
**District:** Queenstown, Dempsey Hill
**Address:** 13A Dempsey Road
Singapore 247694 Singapore
**Phone:** +65 6476 2922

#174
**Roomful of Blues**
Pub
**Average price:** Moderate
**District:** Bencoolen
**Address:** 72 Prinsep St
Singapore 188671 Singapore
**Phone:** +65 6837 0882

#175
**La Viva**
Bar
**Average price:** Moderate
**District:** Bras Brasah
**Address:** 01-13 Chijmes
Singapore 187996 Singapore
**Phone:** +65 6339 4290

#176
**Mariko's**
Cocktail Bar
**Average price:** Moderate
**District:** Chinatown
**Address:** 4 Jiak Chuan Road
Singapore 089261 Singapore
**Phone:** +65 6221 8262

#177
**O'learys Bar & Grill**
Bar
**Average price:** Moderate
**District:** City Hall
**Address:** 30 Raffles Avenue, #01-04
Singapore Flyer
Singapore 039804 Singapore
**Phone:** +65 6337 6718

#178
**Baden**
Bar
**Average price:** Moderate
**District:** Holland Village
**Address:** 42 Lorong Mambong
Holland Village, 277696 Singapore
**Phone:** +65 6463 8127

#179
**Harry's Bar**
Bar
**Average price:** Moderate
**District:** Raffles Place
**Address:** 30 Robinson Rd
Singapore 048546 Singapore
**Phone:** +65 6324 8076

#180
**Forbidden City/Bar**
Bar
**Average price:** Moderate
**District:** Clarke Quay
**Address:** 3a Merchant Court
Singapore 179020 Singapore
**Phone:** +65 6557 6272

#181
**Barber Shop by Timbre**
Bar, Pizza, Music Venue
**Average price:** Moderate
**District:** City Hall
**Address:** 1 Old Parliament Lane
Singapore 179429 Singapore
**Phone:** +65 6336 3386

#182
**eM Studio**
Bar
**Average price:** Moderate
**District:** Robertson Quay
**Address:** 1 Nanson Rd
Singapore 238909 Singapore
**Phone:** +65 6849 8686

#183
**Harry's Bar**
Bar
**Average price:** Inexpensive
**District:** Holland Village
**Address:** 27 Lorong Mambong
Singapore 277686 Singapore
**Phone:** +65 6467 4222

#184
**Chamber Food & Entertainment**
Pub, Food, Art & Entertainment
**Average price:** Moderate
**District:** Arab Street, Bugis
**Address:** 11 Unity St
Singapore 237995 Singapore
**Phone:** +65 6738 1332

#185
**Woobar**
Cocktail Bar
**Average price:** Expensive
**District:** Sentosa
**Address:** 21 Ocean Way
Singapore 098374 Singapore
**Phone:** +65 6808 7258

#186
**Wine Bos**
Wine Bar, American
**Average price:** Moderate
**District:** Arab Street
**Address:** 787 North Bridge Road
Singapore 198755 Singapore
**Phone:** +65 6538 7886

#187
**Molly Roffey's Irish Pub**
Pub, American
**Average price:** Moderate
**District:** Bras Brasah, Dhoby Ghaut
**Address:** 51 Bras Basah Road
Singapore 189554 Singapore
**Phone:** +65 6238 0989

#188
**Robolots**
Bar, Creperies
**Average price:** Moderate
**District:** Joo Chiat
**Address:** 451 Joo Chiat Rd
Singapore 427664 Singapore
**Phone:** +65 6345 0080

#189
**PERFECTO Fusion**
Bar, Asian Fusion
**Average price:** Expensive
**District:** Raffles Place
**Address:** 3 Pickering Street
Singapore 048660 Singapore
**Phone:** +65 9144 0162

#190
**Harry's**
Bar
**Average price:** Moderate
**District:** Raffles Place
**Address:** 39 Pekin St
Singapore 048769 Singapore
**Phone:** +65 6536 1948

#191
**Paradiso Restaurant and Bar**
Bar, Latin American
**Average price:** Moderate
**District:** Sentosa
**Address:** 31 Ocean Way
Singapore 098375 Singapore
**Phone:** +65 6694 5428

#192
**Brewbaker's Kitchen & Bar**
Bar
**Average price:** Moderate
**District:** Sengkang
**Address:** 01-06 Anchorvale
Community Club, 544965 Singapore
**Phone:** +65 6886 1811

#193
**The Rupee Room**
Bar
**Average price:** Moderate
**District:** Clarke Quay
**Address:** 01-15 Clarke Quay
Singapore 179021 Singapore
**Phone:** +65 6334 2455

#194
**La Maison Du Whisky**
Bar
**Average price:** Expensive
**District:** Robertson Quay
**Address:** 80 Mohamed Sultan Rd
Singapore 239013 Singapore
**Phone:** +65 6733 0059

#195
**Lazy Lizard**
Bar
**Average price:** Moderate
**District:** Sixth Avenue, Bukit Timah
**Address:** 2 Sixth Ave
Singapore 276470 Singapore
**Phone:** +65 6468 6289

#196
**Heat Ultralounge**
Bar
**Average price:** Moderate
**District:** Tanglin
**Address:** 2f Royal Plz On Scotts
Singapore 228220 Singapore
**Phone:** +65 6589 7722

#197
**Bernie's Restaurant and Bar**
Bar, Burgers
**Average price:** Moderate
**District:** Changi
**Address:** 961a Upper Changi Rd North
Singapore 507663 Singapore
**Phone:** +65 6542 2232

#198
**Nueva Cuba**
Bar
**Average price:** Moderate
**District:** Bayfront, Raffles Place
**Address:** 70 Collyer Quay
Singapore 049323 Singapore
**Phone:** +65 6535 0538

#199
**The Trenchard Arms**
Pub
**Average price:** Moderate
**District:** Joo Chiat, Marine Parade
**Address:** 47 East Coast Rd
Singapore 428767 Singapore
**Phone:** +65 6344 0912

#200
**Bibi Bar**
Bar
**Average price:** Moderate
**District:** Dhoby Ghaut, Orchard
**Address:** 53 Orchard Road
Singapore 4536 Singapore
**Phone:** +65 3636 3722

# TOP 285 NIGHTLIFE

Recommended by Locals & Trevelers

(From #1 to #285)

#1
## The Good Beer Company
Bar, Street Vendor
**Average price:** Moderate
**District:** Chinatown
**Address:** 335 Smith Street
Singapore 050335 Singapore
**Phone: +65 9430 2750**

#2
## National Library
Museum, Educational Service,
Library
**Average price:** Moderate
**District:** Bugis, Bras Brasah
**Address:** 100 Victoria Street
Singapore 188064 Singapore
**Phone:** +65 6332 3225

#3
## Maison Ikkoku
Cafe, Coffee & Tea, Cocktail Bar
**Average price:** Expensive
**District:** Arab Street
**Address:** 20 Kandahar Street
Singapore 198885 Singapore
**Phone:** +65 6294 0078

#4
## Artichoke Cafe & Bar
Bar, Cafe
**Average price:** Expensive
**District:** Bencoolen
**Address:** 161 Middle Rd
Singapore 188977 Singapore
**Phone:** +65 6336 6949

#5
## 28 Hong Kong Street
Bar
**Average price:** Exclusive
**District:** Clarke Quay
**Address:** 28 HongKong Street
Singapore 059667 Singapore
**Phone:** +65 6533 2001

#6
## Jigger and Pony
Cocktail Bar
**Average price:** Exclusive
**District:** Tanjong Pagar
**Address:** 101 Amoy Street
Singapore 069921 Singapore
**Phone:** +65 6223 9101

#7
## Zouk
Dance Club, Wine Bar
**Average price:** Expensive
**District:** River Valley
**Address:** 17 Jiak Kim Street
Singapore 169420 Singapore
**Phone:** +65 6738 2988

#8
## Going Om
Bar, Cafe
**Average price:** Expensive
**District:** Arab Street
**Address:** 63 Haji Lane
Singapore 189256 Singapore
**Phone:** +65 6297 9197

#9
## Ippudo x Tao
Food, Japanese, Bar
**Average price:** Expensive
**District:** Robertson Quay
**Address:** 207 River Valley Road
Singapore 238275 Singapore
**Phone:** +65 6887 5315

#10
## Bar Stories
Bar
**Average price:** Exclusive
**District:** Arab Street
**Address:** 55/57A Haji Lane
Singapore 189248 Singapore
**Phone:** +65 6298 0838

#11
## Bitters & Love
Champagne Bar
**Average price:** Expensive
**District:** Clarke Quay
**Address:** 36 North Canal Road
Singapore 059292 Singapore
**Phone:** +65 6438 1836

#12
## Ice Cold Beer
Bar
**Average price:** Expensive
**District:** Somerset, Orchard
**Address:** 9 Emerald Hill Road
Singapore 229293 Singapore
**Phone:** +65 6735 9929

#14
## Wala Wala Cafe Bar
Bar
**Average price:** Expensive
**District:** Holland Village
**Address:** 31 Lorong Mambong
Singapore 277689 Singapore
**Phone:** +65 6462 4288

#15
## Cicheti
Wine Bar, Italian, Pizza
**Average price:** Moderate
**District:** Arab Street
**Address:** 52 Kandahar Street
Singapore 198901 Singapore
**Phone:** +65 6292 5012

#16
## No. 5
Bar
**Average price:** Expensive
**District:** Somerset, Orchard
**Address:** 5 Emerald Hill Road
Singapore 229289 Singapore
**Phone:** +65 6732 0818

#17
## 1-Altitude Gallery & Bar
Wine Bar, Lounge, Wineries
**Average price:** Exclusive
**District:** Raffles Place
**Address:** 1 Raffles Place
Singapore 048616 Singapore
**Phone:** +65 6438 0410

#18
## Brewerkz
Bar
**Average price:** Exclusive
**District:** Clarke Quay
**Address:** 30 Merchant Road
Singapore 058282 Singapore
**Phone:** +65 6438 7438

#19
## Lagnaa Barefoot Dining
Indian, Lounge, Fondue
**Average price:** Exclusive
**District:** Little India
**Address:** 6 Upper Dickson Road
Singapore 207466 Singapore
**Phone:** +65 6296 1215

#20
## JiBiru Craft Beer Bar
Japanese, Bar
**Average price:** Expensive
**District:** Somerset, Orchard
**Address:** 313 Somerset
Singapore 238895 Singapore
**Phone:** +65 6732 6884

#21
## Long Bar
Wine Bar, Cocktail Bar
**Average price:** Exclusive
**District:** Bras Brasah, City Hall
**Address:** 1 Beach Road
Singapore 189673 Singapore
**Phone:** +65 6412 1816

#22
## OverEasy
Bar, Diners, American
**Average price:** Expensive
**District:** Bayfront, Raffles Place
**Address:** 1 Fullerton Rd
Singapore 049213 Singapore
**Phone:** +65 6423 0701

#23
## Praelum Wine Bistro
Wine Bar, Cafe
**Average price:** Exclusive
**District:** Duxton Hill, Tanjong Pagar
**Address:** 4 Duxton Hill
Singapore 089590 Singapore
**Phone:** +65 6238 5287

#24
## Little Part 1
Bar, American
**Average price:** Expensive
**District:** Thomson
**Address:** 15 Jasmine Road
Singapore 576584 Singapore
**Phone:** +65 6451 7553

#25
## 2am: Dessert Bar
Bar, Desserts, Coffee & Tea
**Average price:** Exclusive
**District:** Holland Village
**Address:** 21a Lorong Liput
Singapore 277733 Singapore
**Phone:** +65 6291 9727

#26
## Orihara Shouten
Bar, Japanese
**Average price:** Moderate
**District:** Robertson Quay
**Address:** 11 Unity St
Singapore 237995 Singapore
**Phone:** +65 6836 5710

#27
## Chicken Up
Korean, Fast Food, Pub
**Average price:** Expensive
**District:** Duxton Hill, Tanjong Pagar
**Address:** 48 Tanjong Pagar Road
Singapore 088469 Singapore
**Phone:** +65 6327 1203

#28
## Suprette
Bar, American
**Average price:** Exclusive
**District:** Little India
**Address:** 383 Jalan Besar
Singapore 209001 Singapore
**Phone:** +65 6298 8962

#29
## Cash Studio Family Karaoke Box
Karaoke
**Average price:** Moderate
**District:** Somerset, Orchard
**Address:** 5 Koek Rd
Singapore 228796 Singapore
**Phone:** +65 6533 0090

#30
## Coastes
Bar
**Average price:** Expensive
**District:** Sentosa
**Address:** 50 Siloso Beach Walk
Singapore 099000 Singapore
**Phone:** +65 6274 9668

#31
## Satsuma Shochu Dining Bar
Japanese, Bar
**Average price:** Moderate
**District:** Robertson Quay
**Address:** 1 Nanson Road,
#01-10/#02-10, 238909 Singapore
**Phone:** +65 6235 3565

#32
## Bedrock Bar & Grill
Bar
**Average price:** Moderate
**District:** Somerset, Orchard
**Address:** 01-05 Pan Pacific Serviced
Suites
Singapore 238163 Singapore
**Phone:** +65 6238 0054

#33
## The Coastal Settlement
Bar, Breakfast & Brunch
**Average price:** Exclusive
**District:** Changi
**Address:** 200 Netheravon Road
Singapore 508529 Singapore
**Phone:** +65 6475 0200

#34
## Tanjong Beach Club
Bar
**Average price:** Exclusive
**District:** Sentosa
**Address:** 120 Tanjong Bch Walk
Singapore 098942 Singapore
**Phone:** +65 6270 1355

#35
## The Naked Finn
Seafood, Pub
**Average price:** Exclusive
**District:** Alexandra
**Address:** 41 Malan Road
Singapore 109454 Singapore
**Phone:** +65 6694 0807

#36
## The Spiffy Dapper
Cocktail Bar
**Average price:** Expensive
**District:** Boat Quay
**Address:** 2/F 61 Boat Quay
Singapore 049849 Singapore
**Phone:** +65 8233 9810

#37
## Standing Sushi Bar
Japanese, Bar, Sushi Bar
**Average price:** Expensive
**District:** Bras Brasah
**Address:** 8 Queen Street
Singapore 188535 Singapore
**Phone:** +65 6333 1335

#38
## Café Iguana
Lounge, Tapas, Mexican
**Average price:** Expensive
**District:** Clarke Quay
**Address:** 30 Merchant Rd
Singapore 058282 Singapore
**Phone:** +65 6236 1275

#39
## Orchard Tower
Hotel, Dance Club
**Average price:** Expensive
**District:** Tanglin
**Address:** Orchard Rd 400
Singapore 238875 Singapore
**Phone:** +65 6734 6619

#40
## B28
Jazz & Blues, Lounge
**Average price:** Exclusive
**District:** Ann Siang Hill, Tanjong Pagar
**Address:** 28 Ann Siang Road
Singapore 069708 Singapore
**Phone:** +65 9026 3466

#41
## Mr Punch
Pub, Food, Museum
**Average price:** Moderate
**District:** Bugis, Bras Brasah, City Hall
**Address:** 26 Seah Street
Singapore 188382 Singapore
**Phone:** +65 6334 5155

#42
## Paulaner Bräuhaus Singapore
Bar, Cafe
**Average price:** Expensive
**District:** City Hall
**Address:** 9 Raffles Boulevard
Singapore 039596 Singapore
**Phone:** +65 6883 2572

#43
## KU DÉ TA
Bar, Asian Fusion
**Average price:** Exclusive
**District:** Bayfront
**Address:** 1 Bayfront Avenue Marina
Singapore 018971 Singapore
**Phone:** +65 6688 7688

#44
**Hood Bar and Cafe**
Bar, Cafe
**Average price:** Moderate
**District:** Bugis
**Address:** 201 Victoria Street
Singapore 188067 Singapore
**Phone:** +65 6221 8846

#45
**Chihuly Lounge**
Bar
**Average price:** Exclusive
**District:** City Hall
**Address:** 7 Raffles Ave
Singapore 039799 Singapore
**Phone:** +65 6434 5288

#46
**LeVeL33**
Bar, GastroPub
**Average price:** Exclusive
**District:** Bayfront
**Address:** 8 Marina Boulevard #33-01
Singapore 018981 Singapore
**Phone:** +65 6834 3133

#47
**Tanuki Raw**
Japanese, Lounge, Sushi Bar
**Average price:** Expensive
**District:** Somerset, Orchard
**Address:** 181 Orchard Road
Singapore 238896 Singapore
**Phone:** +65 6636 5949

#48
**Nassim Hill**
Bar, Cafe, Bakeries
**Average price:** Expensive
**District:** Tanglin
**Address:** 56 Tanglin Road #01-03
Tanglin Post Office
Singapore 247964 Singapore
**Phone:** +65 6835 1128

#49
**Timbre Substation**
Restaurant, Bar
**Average price:** Expensive
**District:** Bras Basah, Dhoby Ghaut
**Address:** 45 Armenian Street
Singapore 179936 Singapore
**Phone:** +65 6338 8030

#50
**The Bar at Morton's**
Lounge, Cocktail Bar
**Average price:** Expensive
**District:** City Hall
**Address:** 5 Raffles Avenue
Singapore 039797 Singapore
**Phone:** +65 6339 3740

#51
**Crazy Elephant**
Bar
**Average price:** Exclusive
**District:** Clarke Quay
**Address:** 01-07 Clarke Quay
Singapore 179024 Singapore
**Phone:** +65 6337 1990

#52
**Sabio Tapas Bar**
Spanish, Bar
**Average price:** Exclusive
**District:** Duxton Hill, Tanjong Pagar
**Address:** 5 Duxton Hill
Singapore 089591 Singapore
**Phone:** +65 6690 7562

#53
**The White Rabbit**
Bar, European
**Average price:** Exclusive
**District:** Queenstown
**Address:** 39C Harding Rd
Singapore 249541 Singapore
**Phone:** +65 9721 0536

#54
**The Crazy Elephant**
Jazz & Blues, Music Venue
**Average price:** Moderate
**District:** Clarke Quay
**Address:** River Valley Road 3E
Singapore 179024 Singapore
**Phone:** +65 6337 7859

#55
**Smith Street Taps**
Pub
**Average price:** Moderate
**District:** Chinatown
**Address:** Blk 335 Smith Street
Chinatown Complex, Singapore 050335
**Phone:** +65 9430 2750

#56
**Changi Village**
Ethnic Food, Pub, Asian Fusion
**Average price:** Moderate
**District:** Changi
**Address:** 1 Netheravon Road
Singapore 508502 Singapore
**Phone:** +65 6379 7111

#57
**Cable Car 1890's Saloon Bar**
Bar
**Average price:** Moderate
**District:** Somerset, Orchard
**Address:** 49 Cuppage Road
Singapore 229466 Singapore
**Phone:** +65 6835 3545

#58
## Fern & Kiwi
Sports Bar
**Average price:** Exclusive
**District:** Clarke Quay
**Address:** 3C River Valley Rd
Singapore 179024 Singapore
**Phone:** +65 6336 2271

#59
## Garibaldi Italian Restaurant & Bar
Bar, Italian, European
**Average price:** Exclusive
**District:** Bugis, Bras Brasah, City Hall
**Address:** 36 Purvis Street
Singapore 188613 Singapore
**Phone:** +65 6837 1468

#60
## Fordham & Grand
Bar
**Average price:** Expensive
**District:** Tanjong Pagar
**Address:** 43 Craig Road
Singapore 089681 Singapore
**Phone:** +65 6221 3088

#61
## Boomarang Bistro & Bar
Bar, Breakfast & Brunch
**Average price:** Expensive
**District:** Robertson Quay
**Address:** 01-15 The Quayside
Singapore 238252 Singapore
**Phone:** +65 6738 1077

#62
## Tantric
Gay Bar
**Average price:** Moderate
**District:** Chinatown
**Address:** 78 Neil Road
Singapore 088841 Singapore
**Phone:** +65 9245 8556

#63
## Wine Connection Bar & Bistro
Wine Bar
**Average price:** Moderate
**District:** Somerset, Orchard
**Address:** 41 Cuppage Road
Singapore 229462 Singapore
**Phone:** +65 6836 9069

#64
## Fandango Tapas & Wine Bar
Bar, Tapas
**Average price:** Exclusive
**District:** Bras Brasah
**Address:** 30 Victoria Street
Singapore 187996 Singapore
**Phone:** +65 6333 3450

#65
## Chit's Bar and Restaurant
Diners, Bar
**Average price:** Expensive
**District:** Changi
**Address:** 11 Changi Coast Walk
Singapore 499740 Singapore
**Phone:** +65 6214 9168

#66
## Lot, Stock & Barrel Pub
Pub
**Average price:** Moderate
**District:** Bras Brasah, City Hall
**Address:** 30 Seah Street
Singapore 188386 Singapore
**Phone:** +65 6338 5540

#67
## Muddy Murphy's
Pub, Irish
**Average price:** Expensive
**District:** Tanglin
**Address:** 111 Somerset Road
Singapore 238879 Singapore
**Phone:** +65 6735 0400

#68
## The Halia At Raffles Hotel
Cocktail Bar, Asian Fusion
**Average price:** Exclusive
**District:** Bras Brasah, City Hall
**Address:** 1 Beach Road
Singapore 189673 Singapore
**Phone:** +65 9639 1148

#69
## Fatboy's The Burger Bar
Bar, Burgers
**Average price:** Expensive
**District:** Thomson
**Address:** 187 Upper Thomson Rd
Singapore 574335 Singapore
**Phone:** +65 6252 8780

#70
## Hombre Cantina
Mexican, Bar
**Average price:** Moderate
**District:** Boat Quay
**Address:** 53 Boat Quay
Singapore 049842 Singapore
**Phone:** +65 6438 6708

#71
## Wharf Oyster Bar & Grill
Seafood, Bar
**Average price:** Exclusive
**District:** Robertson Quay
**Address:** 60 Robertson Quay
Singapore 238252 Singapore
**Phone:** +65 6235 2466

#72
**The Black Swan**
Bar, Bistro
**Average price:** Exclusive
**District:** Raffles Place
**Address:** 19 Cecil Street
Singapore 049704 Singapore
**Phone:** +65 8181 3305

#73
**The Cider Pit**
Pub
**Average price:** Moderate
**District:** Joo Chiat
**Address:** 328 Joo Chiat Road
Singapore 427585 Singapore
**Phone:** +65 6440 0504

#74
**Pangaea**
Dance Club
**Average price:** Exclusive
**District:** Bayfront
**Address:** 2 Bayfront Ave
Singapore 018956 Singapore
**Phone:** +65 6688 7448

#75
**Brussels Sprouts**
Pub, Belgian
**Average price:** Moderate
**District:** Robertson Quay
**Address:** 80 Mohamed Sultan Road
Singapore 239013 Singapore
**Phone:** +65 6887 4344

#76
**Colbar - Colonial Bar**
Bar, Local Flavor
**Average price:** Exclusive
**District:** Wessex Estate
**Address:** 9A Whitchurch Rd
Singapore 138839 Singapore
**Phone:** +65 6779 4859

#77
**Bar Bar Black Sheep**
Bar, Cafe
**Average price:** Moderate
**District:** Sixth Avenue, Bukit Timah
**Address:** 879 Cherry Avenue
Singapore 279892 Singapore
**Phone:** +65 6468 9382

#78
**Tawandang Microbrewery**
Bar, Thai, Beer, Wine & Spirits
**Average price:** Exclusive
**District:** Queenstown, Dempsey Hill
**Address:** 26 Dempsey Rd
Singapore 249686 Singapore
**Phone:** +65 6476 6742

#79
**Rokeby**
Bistro, Cafe, Bar
**Average price:** Expensive
**District:** Serangoon
**Address:** 15-9 Jalan Riang
Singapore 358972 Singapore
**Phone:** +65 9106 0437

#80
**Nektar**
Bar
**Average price:** Moderate
**District:** Newton
**Address:** 31 Scotts Road
Singapore 228225 Singapore
**Phone:** +65 6836 9185

#81
**Brewerkz**
Bar
**Average price:** Expensive
**District:** Kallang
**Address:** 2 Stadium Walk
Singapore 397691 Singapore
**Phone:** +65 6345 9905

#82
**Reddot Brewhouse**
Restaurant, Bar
**Average price:** Expensive
**District:** Queenstown, Dempsey Hill
**Address:** 25a Dempsey Rd
Singapore 247691 Singapore
**Phone:** +65 6475 0500

#83
**Teo Heng KTV Studio**
Karaoke, Music & DVDs
**Average price:** Moderate
**District:** Joo Chiat, Marine Parade
**Address:** 865 Mountbatten Road
Singapore 437844 Singapore
**Phone:** +65 6345 6512

#84
**Cuscaden Patio Cafe & Pub**
Pub
**Average price:** Expensive
**District:** Tanglin
**Address:** 21 Cuscaden Road
Singapore 249720 Singapore
**Phone:** +65 6887 3319

#85
**DARTSoul Cafe & Bar**
Bar
**Average price:** Expensive
**District:** Bugis
**Address:** 201 Victoria Street
Singapore 188067 Singapore
**Phone:** +65 6636 9951

#86
**Caveau**
Wine Bar
**Average price:** Moderate
**District:** Tanglin
**Address:** Shaw Centre 1 Scotts Road
Singapore 358666 Singapore
**Phone:** +65 6737 2622

#87
**Bungy Bar**
Cafe, Pub
**Average price:** Moderate
**District:** Clarke Quay
**Address:** 3E River Valley Road
Singapore 179024 Singapore
**Phone:** +65 6339 5707

#88
**Handlebar**
Bar
**Average price:** Expensive
**District:** Sembawang
**Address:** 57 Jalan Mempurong
Singapore 759057 Singapore
**Phone:** +65 6475 9571

#89
**Stärker Fresh Beer**
Bar
**Average price:** Expensive
**District:** Holland Village
**Address:** 25 Lorong Mambong
Singapore 277684 Singapore
**Phone:** +65 6465 8368

#90
**Cuscaden @ CHIJMES**
Bar
**Average price:** Moderate
**District:** Bras Brasah
**Address:** 30 Victoria Street #01-04
Singapore 187996 Singapore
**Phone:** +65 6338 3510

#91
**Wine Connection**
Wine Bar, Beer, Wine & Spirits
**Average price:** Expensive
**District:** Marine Parade, Katong
**Address:** 112 East Coast Rd
Singapore 428802 Singapore
**Phone:** +65 6346 6588

#92
**Ten Dollar Club Family
K.T.V. Karaoke**
Karaoke
**Average price:** Moderate
**District:** Chinatown
**Address:** 35A Smith Street
Singapore 058948 Singapore
**Phone:** +65 6225 1231

#93
**Piedra Negra**
Mexican, Bar
**Average price:** Expensive
**District:** Arab Street
**Address:** 241 Beach Road
Singapore 189753 Singapore
**Phone:** +65 6291 1297

#94
**Beer Market**
Bar
**Average price:** Exclusive
**District:** Clarke Quay
**Address:** 3B River Valley Road
Singapore 179021 Singapore
**Phone:** +65 9661 8283

#95
**Mink**
Dance Club
**Average price:** Moderate
**District:** City Hall
**Address:** 7 Raffles Blvd
Pan Pacific Hotel, 039595 Singapore
**Phone:** +65 6374 0205

#96
**Attica**
Bar
**Average price:** Expensive
**District:** Clarke Quay
**Address:** 3A River Valley Rd
Singapore 179020 Singapore
**Phone:** +65 6333 9973

#97
**Jewel Cafe + Bar**
Coffee & Tea, Bar, Breakfast & Brunch
**Average price:** Expensive
**District:** Farrer Park
**Address:** 129 Rangoon Road
Singapore 218407 Singapore
**Phone:** +65 6298 9216

#98
**Immigrants**
Bar
**Average price:** Exclusive
**District:** Joo Chiat
**Address:** 467 Joo Chiat Road
Singapore 427678 Singapore
**Phone:** +65 8511 7322

#99
**PigsFly Kitchen & Bar**
Diners, Bar
**Average price:** Expensive
**District:** Newton, Novena
**Address:** 1 Goldhill Plaza
Singapore 308899 Singapore
**Phone:** +65 6356 8592

#100
**The New Harbour Cafe & Bar**
Bar, Cafe
**Average price:** Moderate
**District:** Duxton Hill, Tanjong Pagar
**Address:** 114 Tanjong Pagar Road
Singapore 088529 Singapore
**Phone:** +65 6226 2657

#101
**Harry's**
Bar
**Average price:** Moderate
**District:** Bayfront, City Hall
**Address:** 8 Raffles Ave
Singapore 039802 Singapore
**Phone:** +65 6334 0132

#102
**China One**
Bar, Dance Club
**Average price:** Expensive
**District:** Lavender
**Address:** Block 3E River Valley Road
Singapore 179024 Singapore
**Phone:** +65 6339 0280

#103
**Sidewalk Tavern**
Pub
**Average price:** Expensive
**District:** Siglap
**Address:** 924 East Coast Rd
Singapore 459115 Singapore
**Phone:** +65 6448 5979

#104
**Barkode Cocktail Bar**
Bar
**Average price:** Moderate
**District:** Little India
**Address:** 66 Dunlop St
Singapore 209394 Singapore
**Phone:** +65 6396 4463

#105
**Bar 83**
Bar
**Average price:** Moderate
**District:** Ann Siang Hill, Tanjong Pagar
**Address:** 83 Club Street
Singapore 069451 Singapore
**Phone:** +65 6220 4083

#106
**Eight**
European, Wine Bar, Asian Fusion
**Average price:** Exclusive
**District:** Chinatown
**Address:** 8 Bukit Pasoh Road
Singapore 089822 Singapore
**Phone:** +65 6220 4513

#107
**Keyaki**
Bar, Japanese
**Average price:** Moderate
**District:** City Hall
**Address:** 7 Raffles Blvd
Singapore 039595 Singapore
**Phone:** +65 6826 8240

#108
**The Penny Black**
Art& Entertainment, Pub
**Average price:** Expensive
**District:** Raffles Place, Boat Quay
**Address:** 27 Boat Quay
Singapore 049817 Singapore
**Phone:** +65 6538 2300

#109
**Wabar**
Bar
**Average price:** Expensive
**District:** Duxton Hill, Tanjong Pagar
**Address:** 62 Tanjong Pagar Road
Singapore 088483 Singapore
**Phone:** +65 6224 7073

#110
**The Old Brown Shoe**
Pub
**Average price:** Expensive
**District:** Bukit Timah
**Address:** 619f Bukit Timah Road
Singapore 269726 Singapore
**Phone:** +65 6468 4626

#111
**5 Izakaya Bar**
Bar
**Average price:** Expensive
**District:** Bayfront, Raffles Place
**Address:** 16 Collyer Quay
Singapore 049318 Singapore
**Phone:** +65 6536 8955

#112
**The Vault**
Bar, Music Venue
**Average price:** Exclusive
**District:** Boat Quay
**Address:** 23 Circular Road
Singapore 049379 Singapore
**Phone:** +65 6223 9695

#113
**Owls Brew**
Pub, GastroPub
**Average price:** Expensive
**District:** Mount Sophia
**Address:** 146 MacKenzie Road
Singapore 228723 Singapore
**Phone:** +65 6333 3440

#114
**Little Saigon**
Vietnamese, Pub, Ethnic Food
**Average price:** Exclusive
**District:** Clarke Quay
**Address:** Blk E River Valley Road
Singapore 179024 Singapore
**Phone:** +65 6337 5585

#115
**Fuse**
Bar, Cafe
**Average price:** Exclusive
**District:** Bayfront
**Address:** 8 Bayfront Avenue
Singapore 018955 Singapore
**Phone:** +65 6688 5529

#116
**Owl Bar**
Bar
**Average price:** Moderate
**District:** Outram
**Address:** 2 College Road
Singapore 169850 Singapore
**Phone:** +65 9299 6898

#117
**The Blooie's Roadhouse Bar&Grill**
Art& Entertainment, Lounge, Pub,
Restaurant
**Average price:** Moderate
**District:** Kent Ridge, Pasir Panjang
**Address:** 21 Science Park Road #01-01
Singapore 117628 Singapore
**Phone:** +65 6775 0446

#118
**OChre**
Bar, Italian
**Average price:** Exclusive
**District:** Somerset, Orchard
**Address:** 181 Orchard Rd
Singapore 238896 Singapore
**Phone:** +65 6634 0423

#119
**Jiu Zhuang**
Lounge, Asian Fusion
**Average price:** Exclusive
**District:** Queenstown, Dempsey Hill
**Address:** 6D Dempsey Road
Singapore 247664 Singapore
**Phone:** +65 6471 1711

#120
**Atrium**
Lounge
**Average price:** Moderate
**District:** City Hall
**Address:** 7 Raffles Blvd
Singapore 039595 Singapore
**Phone:** +65 6826 8240

#121
**ZZAPI**
Pizza, Bar
**Average price:** Expensive
**District:** River Valley
**Address:** 491 River Valley Road
Singapore 248371 Singapore
**Phone:** +65 6737 3718

#122
**Loof**
Bar
**Average price:** Expensive
**District:** Bugis, Bras Brasah
**Address:** 03-07 Odeon Towers
Ext Rooftop, 188720 Singapore
**Phone:** +65 6338 8035

#123
**Fight Comic Singapore**
Comedy Club, Performing Art
**Average price:** Moderate
**District:** Arab Street
**Address:** 11 Bali Lane
Singapore 189848 Singapore
**Phone:** +65 9007 5651

#124
**K Suites**
Bar, Karaoke
**Average price:** Moderate
**District:** Bugis
**Address:** 201 Victoria Street
Singapore 188067 Singapore
**Phone:** +65 6243 3113

#125
**Ambrosia**
Pub
**Average price:** Moderate
**District:** Arab Street
**Address:** 19 Baghdad St
Singapore 199658 Singapore
**Phone:** +65 6292 7313

#126
**The Tippling Club**
Bar
**Average price:** Expensive
**District:** Duxton Hill, Tanjong Pagar
**Address:** 38 Tanjong Pagar Road
Singapore 088461 Singapore
**Phone:** +65 6475 2217

#127
**DYMK**
Gay Bar
**Average price:** Moderate
**District:** Duxton Hill, Tanjong Pagar
**Address:** 41 Neil Road
Singapore 088824 Singapore
**Phone:** +65 6224 3965

#128
**The Handlebar**
American, Bar
**Average price:** Expensive
**District:** Bayfront, Raffles Place
**Address:** Lock Road 01-01 Singapore
**Phone:** +65 6475 9571

#129
**Wine Connection @ Anchorpoint**
Wine Bar
**Average price:** Moderate
**District:** Queenstown, Alexandra
**Address:** 370 Alexandra Road, #B1-08
Singapore 159953 Singapore
**Phone:** +65 6476 8997

#130
**Mansion Bay**
Dance Club, Bar
**Average price:** Moderate
**District:** Bayfront, City Hall
**Address:** 8 Raffles Avenue
Singapore 039802 Singapore
**Phone:** +65 6333 4083

#131
**Teo Heng KTV Studio**
Karaoke
**Average price:** Moderate
**District:** Bencoolen, Orchard
**Address:** 9 Bras Basah Road #02-03
Rendezvous Hotel Gallery Museum
Singapore 189559 Singapore
**Phone:** +65 6338 0603

#132
**Charlie's Tapas Grill & Bar**
Sports Bar, Spanish
**Average price:** Moderate
**District:** Raffles Place, Boat Quay
**Address:** 32 Boat Quay
Singapore 049821 Singapore
**Phone:** +65 6533 5880

#133
**Executive Lounge
Changi Village Hotel**
Lounge
**Average price:** Moderate
**District:** Changi
**Address:** 1 Netheravon Road
Singapore 508502 Singapore
**Phone:** +65 6379 7111

#134
**The Wine Company**
Wine Bar
**Average price:** Expensive
**District:** Sentosa
**Address:** 6 Sentosa Gateway
Singapore 098072 Singapore
**Phone:** +65 6376 9029

#135
**Raffles Place Bistro**
Cafe, Lounge
**Average price:** Moderate
**District:** Bayfront, Raffles Place
**Address:** 2 Marina Boulevard
Singapore 018987 Singapore
**Phone:** +65 6222 6650

#136
**Orchard Towers**
Shopping, Adult Entertainment,
Music Venue
**Average price:** Exclusive
**District:** Tanglin
**Address:** 400 Orchard Road
Singapore 238875 Singapore
**Phone:** +65 6733 7508

#137
**The Butter Factory**
Dance Club, Bar
**Average price:** Exclusive
**District:** Bayfront, Raffles Place
**Address:** 1 Fullerton Square
Singapore 049213 Singapore
**Phone:** +65 6333 8243

#138
**KPO Cafe Bar**
Bar
**Average price:** Expensive
**District:** Somerset, Orchard
**Address:** 1 Killiney Rd
Singapore 239518 Singapore
**Phone:** +65 6733 3648

#139
**Highlander Bar**
Bar
**Average price:** Expensive
**District:** Clarke Quay
**Address:** 3B River Valley Road
Singapore 179021 Singapore
**Phone:** +65 6235 9528

#140
**Park**
Pub, Bistro, Delicatessen
**Average price:** Expensive
**District:** Holland Village
**Address:** 281 Holland Avenue
Singapore 278621 Singapore
**Phone:** +65 9183 4224

#141
**Orgo Bar and Lab**
Restaurant, Bar
**Average price:** Moderate
**District:** City Hall
**Address:** 8 Raffles Avenue, #04-01
Singapore 038982 Singapore
**Phone:** +65 6336 9366

#142
**JJ Atlante**
Dive Bar, Music Venue
**Average price:** Moderate
**District:** Duxton Hill, Tanjong Pagar
**Address:** 39A Duxton Rd
Singapore 089503 Singapore
**Phone:** +65 6225 6225

#143
**The Pit Restaurant & Bar**
Bar, Restaurant
**Average price:** Expensive
**District:** Holland Village
**Address:** 21 Lorong Liput Holland Vlg
Singapore 277736 Singapore
**Phone:** +65 6468 3468

#144
**The Pump Room**
Restaurant, Music Venue
**Average price:** Expensive
**District:** Clarke Quay
**Address:** 3b River Valley Rd
Singapore 179021 Singapore
**Phone:** +65 6334 2628

#145
**Drink Culture**
Beer, Wine & Spirits, Lounge
**Average price:** Moderate
**District:** Chinatown
**Address:** 51 Kreta Ayer Rd
Singapore 089008 Singapore
**Phone:** +65 6557 0538

#146
**Esmirada**
Bar
**Average price:** Exclusive
**District:** Tanglin
**Address:** 442 Orch Rd
Singapore 238879 Singapore
**Phone:** +65 6735 3476

#147
**New Asia**
Lounge
**Average price:** Moderate
**District:** Bras Brasah, City Hall
**Address:** 2 Stamford Road
Singapore 178882 Singapore
**Phone:** +65 6338 8585

#148
**Halo Rooftop Lounge**
Bar
**Average price:** Moderate
**District:** Lavender
**Address:** 231 Outram Road
Singapore 169040 Singapore
**Phone:** +65 6595 1380

#149
**Hannibal European Grill & Bar**
Pizza, Lounge, European
**Average price:** Exclusive
**District:** Robertson Quay
**Address:** 80 Mohamed Sultan Road,
The Pier at Robertson Walk
Singapore 237995 Singapore
**Phone:** +65 6732 7550

#150
**Prelude Rooftop Bar**
Bar
**Average price:** Moderate
**District:** Bayfront, Raffles Place
**Address:** 3 Fullerton Rd #04-01
Singapore 049215 Singapore
**Phone:** +65 6538 9038

#151
**K Box**
Karaoke
**Average price:** Moderate
**District:** Somerset, Orchard
**Address:** 2 Orchard Link
Singapore 237978 Singapore
**Phone:** +65 6755 3113

#152
**i DArt Senso Bar**
Pub
**Average price:** Exclusive
**District:** Robertson Quay
**Address:** 27 Mohamed Sultan Road
Singapore 238971 Singapore
**Phone:** +65 6737 3162

#153
**Lobby Court**
Bar
**Average price:** Moderate
**District:** Tanglin
**Address:** 22 Orange Grv Rd
Singapore 258350 Singapore
**Phone:** +65 6431 6156

#154
**Celina's GastroBar**
Bar
**Average price:** Moderate
**District:** Duxton Hill, Tanjong Pagar
**Address:** 51 Duxton Road
Singapore 089515 Singapore
**Phone:** +65 6220 1684

#155
**OKB**
Wine Bar, Bakeries
**Average price:** Moderate
**District:** Chinatown
**Address:** 1 Kampong Bahru Road
Singapore 169339 Singapore
**Phone:** +65 6220 4711

#156
## Porterhouse - Grill & Bar
Bar, American
**Average price:** Moderate
**District:** Somerset
**Address:** 113 Killiney Road
Singapore 239550 Singapore
**Phone:** +65 6732 5113

#157
## Taboo Cafe & Bar
Bar, Dance Club
**Average price:** Moderate
**District:** Tanjong Pagar, Chinatown
**Address:** 65 Neil Road
Singapore 088897 Singapore
**Phone:** +65 6225 6256

#158
## Balaclava
Pub, Music Venue
**Average price:** Exclusive
**District:** Orchard
**Address:** 2 Orchard Turn
Singapore 238801 Singapore
**Phone:** +65 6339 1600

#159
## Molly Malone'S Irish Pub
Cafe, Pub
**Average price:** Moderate
**District:** Raffles Place, Boat Quay
**Address:** 56 Circular Rd
Singapore 049398 Singapore
**Phone:** +65 6536 2029

#160
## Zushi Bar
Bar
**Average price:** Moderate
**District:** Serangoon
**Address:** 301 Serangoon Avenue 2
Singapore 550301 Singapore
**Phone:** +65 6858 4929

#161
## Obama's Irish Pub
Bar
**Average price:** Moderate
**District:** Tanjong Pagar
**Address:** 54 Tras Street Tanjong Pagar
Singapore 078993 Singapore
**Phone:** +65 6225 1090

#162
## Jekyll & Hyde
Cocktail Bar
**Average price:** Moderate
**District:** Tanjong Pagar
**Address:** 49 Tras Street
Singapore 078988 Singapore
**Phone:** +65 6222 3349

#163
## Rasputin
Dance Club, Bar, Russian
**Average price:** Exclusive
**District:** Clarke Quay
**Address:** 3B River Valley Road
Singapore 179021 Singapore
**Phone:** +65 6337 7011

#164
## Manhattan
Cocktail Bar
**Average price:** Moderate
**District:** Tanglin
**Address:** 1 Cuscaden Road
Singapore 249715 Singapore
**Phone:** +65 6725 3377

#165
## Bikini Bar
Bar
**Average price:** Expensive
**District:** Sentosa
**Address:** 50 Siloso Beach Walk
Singapore 099000 Singapore
**Phone:** +65 6276 6070

#166
## Quaruba'r
Bar
**Average price:** Moderate
**District:** Siglap
**Address:** 113 Frankel Avenue
Singapore 458230 Singapore
**Phone:** +65 6243 0113

#167
## Play
Bar, Dance Club
**Average price:** Moderate
**District:** Duxton Hill, Tanjong Pagar
**Address:** 21 Tanjong Pagar Rd
Singapore 088444 Singapore
**Phone:** +65 6227 7400

#168
## Club Nana
Dance Club
**Average price:** Moderate
**District:** Clarke Quay
**Address:** 5 Magazine Road
Singapore 059571 Singapore
**Phone:** +65 6535 3030

#169
## Dallas Restaurant & Bar
American, Bar
**Average price:** Moderate
**District:** Raffles Place, Boat Quay
**Address:** 31 Boat Quay
Singapore 049820 Singapore
**Phone:** +65 6532 2131

#170
**Alley Bar**
Bar, Restaurant
**Average price:** Expensive
**District:** Somerset, Orchard
**Address:** 180 Orchard Road
Singapore 238846 Singapore
**Phone:** +65 6738 8818

#171
**Lucky 13**
Bar, Latin American
**Average price:** Exclusive
**District:** Somerset, Orchard
**Address:** 111 Somerset Road #01-02
TripleOne Somerset
Singapore 238164 Singapore
**Phone:** +65 6733 9800

#172
**Brotzeit German Bier Bar**
Bar, German
**Average price:** Expensive
**District:** Somerset, Orchard
**Address:** 313 Orchard Road
Singapore 238895 Singapore
**Phone:** +65 6834 4038

#173
**Singapore Lyric Opera**
Bar
**Average price:** Moderate
**District:** Bencoolen
**Address:** 155 Waterloo St
Singapore 187962 Singapore
**Phone:** +65 6336 1929

#174
**Victoria Bar**
American, Lounge
**Average price:** Exclusive
**District:** Bugis
**Address:** 80 Middle Rd
Singapore 188966 Singapore
**Phone:** +65 6825 1045

#175
**Kazbar**
Bar
**Average price:** Exclusive
**District:** Raffles Place
**Address:** 01-03 Capital Sq
Singapore 049482 Singapore
**Phone:** +65 6438 2975

#176
**Library@Esplanade**
Bar
**Average price:** Moderate
**District:** Bayfront, City Hall
**Address:** 8 Raffles Ave
Singapore 039802 Singapore
**Phone:** +65 6332 3255

#177
**Asylum Creative**
Bar
**Average price:** Moderate
**District:** Ann Siang Hill, Tanjong Pagar
**Address:** 22A Ann Siang Rd
Singapore 069702 Singapore
**Phone:** +65 6324 2289

#178
**Wiser Karaoke Lounge & Pub**
Pub, Karaoke
**Average price:** Moderate
**District:** Jurong
**Address:** 11 Japanese Garden Road
Singapore 619229 Singapore
**Phone:** +65 6261 1211

#179
**Orgo Bar and Restaurant**
Bar
**Average price:** Expensive
**District:** Bayfront, City Hall
**Address:** #04-01. Roof Terrace
Singapore 039802 Singapore
**Phone:** +65 9733 6911

#180
**Hosted On The Patio**
Mediterranean, Bar
**Average price:** Moderate
**District:** Alexandra
**Address:** 991B Alexandra Road
Singapore 119970 Singapore
**Phone:** +65 6276 7337

#181
**Bar Bar Black Sheep**
Bar
**Average price:** Expensive
**District:** Katong
**Address:** 363 Tanjong Katong Road
Singapore 437121 Singapore
**Phone:** +65 6348 8275

#182
**The Dubliner Irish Pub**
Pub, Art& Entertainment
**Average price:** Expensive
**District:** Somerset, Orchard
**Address:** 165 Penang Rd
Singapore 238461 Singapore
**Phone:** +65 6735 2220

#183
**Quaich Bar at Grand
Copthorne Waterfront**
Bar
**Average price:** Expensive
**District:** River Valley
**Address:** 390A Havelock Road
Singapore 169664 Singapore
**Phone:** +65 6732 3452

#184
**Sara's at Upper Thompson**
Pub
**Average price:** Moderate
**District:** Thomson
**Address:** 217 Upper Thomson Road
Singapore 574350 Singapore
**Phone:** +65 6457 9868

#185
**Vida Vino**
Wine Bar
**Average price:** Exclusive
**District:** Chinatown
**Address:** 29 Keong Saik Road
Singapore 089136 Singapore
**Phone:** +65 6222 1963

#186
**Pind Balluchi Bar & Grill**
Indian, Cocktail Bar, Lounge
**Average price:** Moderate
**District:** Clarke Quay
**Address:** 3B River Valley Road
Singapore 179021 Singapore
**Phone:** +65 6337 7350

#187
**Night & Day**
Bar
**Average price:** Moderate
**District:** Mount Sophia
**Address:** 139 A/c Selegie Rd
Singapore 188309 Singapore
**Phone:** +65 6884 5523

#188
**Señor Santos**
Bar
**Average price:** Moderate
**District:** Clarke Quay
**Address:** 01-12 Clarke Quay
Singapore 179021 Singapore
**Phone:** +65 6336 7741

#189
**Backstage Bar**
Bar
**Average price:** Moderate
**District:** Chinatown
**Address:** 13a Trengganu St
Singapore 058467 Singapore
**Phone:** +65 6392 3913

#190
**Monstercue**
Pool Halls
**Average price:** Moderate
**District:** Dhoby Ghaut, Orchard
**Address:** 100 Orchard Road,
Le Meridien Shopping Centre
Singapore 238840 Singapore
**Phone:** +65 6238 1689

#191
**Resorts World Sentosa
Waterfront Studio**
Music Venue
**Average price:** Moderate
**District:** Sentosa
**Address:** 8 Sentosa Gateway
Singapore 098269 Singapore
**Phone:** +65 6577 8888

#192
**Shi Sheng Claypot Frog Porridge**
Bar, Local Flavor, Street Vendor
**Average price:** Moderate
**District:** Boon Keng
**Address:** 235 Geylang Road
Singapore 389294 Singapore
**Phone:** +65 9083 8180

#193
**Alliance Music Group
AMG Studios**
Music Venue
**Average price:** Moderate
**District:** Lavender
**Address:** 100 Jalan Sultan #02-43
Singapore 199001 Singapore
**Phone:** +65 6392 1868

#194
**&SONS**
Wine Bar, Italian, Bistro
**Average price:** Expensive
**District:** Raffles Place
**Address:** 20 Cross Street, #01-19
Singapore 048422 Singapore
**Phone:** +65 6221 3937

#195
**BRIX**
Bar
**Average price:** Exclusive
**District:** Orchard
**Address:** 10-12 Scotts Road
Singapore 228211 Singapore
**Phone:** +65 6732 1234

#196
**Moosehead Kitchen Bar**
Bar, Tapas
**Average price:** Moderate
**District:** Raffles Place
**Address:** 110 Telok Ayer Street
Singapore 068579 Singapore
**Phone:** +65 6636 8055

#197
**Vie Bar**
Pub
**Average price:** Moderate
**District:** Siglap
**Address:** 914 East Coast Rd
Singapore 459108 Singapore
**Phone:** +65 6245 0010

#198
**L'Aiglon**
Cocktail Bar
**Average price:** Exclusive
**District:** Tanjong Pagar, Chinatown
**Address:** 69 Neil Rd
Singapore 088899 Singapore
**Phone:** +65 6220 0369

#199
**Insomnia**
Bar
**Average price:** Moderate
**District:** Bras Brasah
**Address:** 01-21 Chijmes
Singapore 187996 Singapore
**Phone:** +65 6338 6883

#200
**Relish Singapore Recreation
Club**
Social Club, Party & Event Planning
**Average price:** Expensive
**District:** City Hall
**Address:** B Connaught Drive
Singapore 179682 Singapore
**Phone:** +65 6338 9367

#201
**Super Cue**
Pool Halls
**Average price:** Moderate
**District:** City Hall
**Address:** 03-200 Marina Sq,
6 Raffles Blvd, 039594 Singapore
**Phone:** +65 6334 1000

#202
**Uncabunca**
Pub
**Average price:** Moderate
**District:** Robertson Quay
**Address:** 80 Mohamed Sultan Road
Singapore 239013 Singapore
**Phone:** +65 6735 9848

#203
**Vau Wine Bar**
Cafe, Wineries, Wine Bar
**Average price:** Moderate
**District:** Changi
**Address:** 1 Netheravon Road
Singapore 508502 Singapore
**Phone:** +65 6379 7018

#204
**The Wine Company**
Desserts, Wine Bar, Wineries
**Average price:** Moderate
**District:** Changi
**Address:** 1 Netheravon Road
Singapore 508502 Singapore
**Phone:** +65 6214 0139

#205
**Tang Music Box**
Karaoke
**Average price:** Moderate
**District:** Clarke Quay
**Address:** 3B River Valley Road
#02-03/04 The Foundry
Singapore 179021 Singapore
**Phone:** +65 6338 6659

#206
**Speakeasy**
Bar
**Average price:** Expensive
**District:** Duxton Hill, Tanjong Pagar
**Address:** 50 Tanjong Pagar Road
Singapore 088471 Singapore
**Phone:** +65 9644 9825

#207
**Alegro**
Bar, Spanish
**Average price:** Moderate
**District:** Clarke Quay
**Address:** 01-13 Clarke Quay
Singapore 179023 Singapore
**Phone:** +65 6883 0620

#208
**Bar Bar Black Sheep**
Bar
**Average price:** Expensive
**District:** Robertson Quay
**Address:** 01-04 Robertson Blue
Singapore 238245 Singapore
**Phone:** +65 2009 0511

#209
**Le Noir**
Bar
**Average price:** Moderate
**District:** Clarke Quay
**Address:** 3C River Valley Road
Singapore 179022 Singapore
**Phone:** +65 6339 6365

#210
**Aura**
Dance Club
**Average price:** Moderate
**District:** Newton
**Address:** 442 Orchard Road,
Orchard Hotel, 259800 Singapore
**Phone:** +65 6737 7455

#211
**Ying Yang Rooftop Bar**
Bar
**Average price:** Moderate
**District:** Ann Siang Hill, Tanjong Pagar
**Address:** The Club, 28 Ann Siang Rd
Singapore 069708 Singapore
**Phone:** +65 6808 2188

#212
## Bull & Bear
Bar
**Average price:** Moderate
**District:** Raffles Place
**Address:** 31 Pekin Street
Singapore 048671 Singapore
**Phone:** +65 6557 0879

#213
## District 10 Bar & Restaurant
Bar, Bistro, Coffee & Tea
**Average price:** Exclusive
**District:** Robertson Quay
**Address:** 81 Clemenceau Ave
Singapore 239917 Singapore
**Phone:** +65 6738 4788

#214
## Bartini
Bar
**Average price:** Moderate
**District:** Ann Siang Hill, Tanjong Pagar
**Address:** 46 Club Street
Singapore 069423 Singapore
**Phone:** +65 6221 1025

#215
## Acid Bar
Bar, Music Venue
**Average price:** Expensive
**District:** Somerset, Orchard
**Address:** 180 Orchard Rd
Singapore 238846 Singapore
**Phone:** +65 6738 8828

#216
## Switch
Restaurant, Lounge
**Average price:** Expensive
**District:** Bras Brasah, Orchard
**Address:** 73 Bras Basah Road
Singapore 189556 Singapore
**Phone:** +65 6336 7739

#217
## Aquanova
Bar, Music Venue
**Average price:** Moderate
**District:** Clarke Quay
**Address:** 3 River Valley Rd
Singapore 179022 Singapore
**Phone:** +65 6305 6733

#218
## Brauhaus
German, Pub
**Average price:** Expensive
**District:** Newton, Novena
**Address:** 101 Thomson Rd
Singapore 307591 Singapore
**Phone:** +65 6250 3116

#219
## Octapas Spanish Tapas Bar
Spanish, Bar, Music Venue
**Average price:** Exclusive
**District:** Clarke Quay
**Address:** River Valley Road
Singapore 179023 Singapore
**Phone:** +65 6837 2938

#220
## Mel's Place
Bar
**Average price:** Exclusive
**District:** Marine Parade, Katong
**Address:** 2A Kuo Chuan Avenue
Singapore 426897 Singapore
**Phone:** +65 6440 3573

#221
## Home Club
Dance Club
**Average price:** Moderate
**District:** Clarke Quay
**Address:** 20 Upper Circular Rd
Singapore 058416 Singapore
**Phone:** +65 6538 2928

#222
## Olivia Cassivelaun Fancourt
Cocktail Bar, Lounge, French
**Average price:** Moderate
**District:** City Hall
**Address:** 1 Old Parliament Lane #02-02
Singapore 179429 Singapore
**Phone:** +65 6333 9312

#223
## Actors The Jam Bar
Pub
**Average price:** Moderate
**District:** Boat Quay, Clarke Quay
**Address:** 13a South Bridge Rd
Singapore 058657 Singapore
**Phone:** +65 6535 3270

#224
## St. James Power Station
Bar, Cafe, Coffee & Tea
**Average price:** Expensive
**District:** Harbourfront
**Address:** 3 Sentosa Gtwy
Singapore 098544 Singapore
**Phone:** +65 6270 7676

#225
## F Club
Dance Club
**Average price:** Moderate
**District:** Clarke Quay
**Address:** 38 River Valley Road
Singapore River Singapore
**Phone:** +65 6338 3158

#226
## Forest DArt Cafe & Pub
Pub, Karaoke
**Average price:** Expensive
**District:** Ann Siang Hill, Tanjong Pagar
**Address:** 45 Ann Siang Road
Singapore 069719 Singapore
**Phone:** +65 6227 3522

#227
## K Box
Karaoke
**Average price:** Expensive
**District:** Chinatown
**Address:** 211 New Bridge Rd
Singapore 059432 Singapore
**Phone:** +65 6534 3113

#228
## Prestige Deco Art
Bar
**Average price:** Moderate
**District:** Bugis, Bras Brasah
**Address:** 420 North Brg Rd
Singapore 188727 Singapore
**Phone:** +65 6339 1084

#229
## Hanamco
Pub
**Average price:** Expensive
**District:** Changi
**Address:** Changi Village Rd 5
Singapore 500005 Singapore
**Phone:** +65 6543 1754

#230
## K-Garden Karaoke
Local Flavor, Karaoke
**Average price:** Moderate
**District:** Serangoon Gardens
**Address:** 18A Maju Ave
Singapore 556693 Singapore
**Phone:** +65 6287 7256

#231
## Pub Starlet
Pub
**Average price:** Expensive
**District:** Thomson
**Address:** No.20 Jalan Leban
Singapore 577556 Singapore
**Phone:** +65 6553 0425

#232
## Cow & Coolies Karaoke Pub
Bar, Karaoke
**Average price:** Moderate
**District:** Chinatown
**Address:** 30 Mosque Street
Singapore 059508 Singapore
**Phone:** +65 6221 1239

#233
## Black & White
## Cocktail Bar & Bites
Bar
**Average price:** Moderate
**District:** Robertson Quay
**Address:** 11 Unity Street
Singapore 237995 Singapore
**Phone:** +65 6836 5752

#234
## Koi Sushi and Izakaya
Japanese, Pub
**Average price:** Moderate
**District:** Ann Siang Hill, Tanjong Pagar
**Address:** 89 Club St.
Singapore 069457 Singapore
**Phone:** +65 6225 5915

#235
## Bq Bar
Art& Entertainment, Pub, Restaurant
**Average price:** Moderate
**District:** Boat Quay
**Address:** 39 Boat Quay
Singapore 049828 Singapore
**Phone:** +65 6536 9722

#236
## TBB Tiong Bahru Bar
Wine Bar, GastroPub, Music Venue
**Average price:** Expensive
**District:** Tiong Bahru
**Address:** 3 Seng Poh Road
Singapore 168891 Singapore
**Phone:** +65 6438 4380

#237
## Scarlet City
Karaoke, Dance Club
**Average price:** Moderate
**District:** Ang Mo Kio
**Address:** 53 Ang Mo Kio Avenue 3
#04-01/03, 569933 Singapore
**Phone:** +65 6582 4145

#238
## D-Flat Studios
Musical Instruments, Music Venue
**Average price:** Moderate
**District:** Tiong Bahru
**Address:** 71 Seng Poh Road
Singapore 160071 Singapore
**Phone:** +65 6225 7175

#239
## Oosters
Bar, Belgian
**Average price:** Exclusive
**District:** Raffles Place
**Address:** 25 Church St
Singapore 049482 Singapore
**Phone:** +65 6438 3210

#240
## Fabrika by Chivas 18
Lounge
**Average price:** Moderate
**District:** Keppel, Tanjong Pagar
**Address:** Hoe Chiang Road, Lvl 17
Sky Terrace, Klapsons the Boutique
Hotel
Singapore 089316 Singapore
**Phone:** +65 6521 9029

#241
## Habitat
Bar
**Average price:** Moderate
**District:** Robertson Quay
**Address:** 11 Unity Street #01-10/11
Robertson Walk
Singapore 237995 Singapore
**Phone:** +65 6732 6098

#242
## The Vintage Room
Bar
**Average price:** Moderate
**District:** Duxton Hill, Tanjong Pagar
**Address:** 37 Duxton Hill
Singapore 089615 Singapore
**Phone:** +65 6690 7565

#243
## Harry's
Bar
**Average price:** Expensive
**District:** Queenstown, Dempsey Hill
**Address:** Blk 11 Dempsey Road
Singapore 249673 Singapore
**Phone:** +65 6471 9018

#244
## Flying Hog Cafe & Bar
Bar, Cafe
**Average price:** Moderate
**District:** Duxton Hill, Tanjong Pagar
**Address:** 32A Duxton Rd
Singapore 089496 Singapore
**Phone:** +65 6327 1518

#245
## Beach Cabana
Bar
**Average price:** Moderate
**District:** Marine Parade
**Address:** 1000 East Coast Pkwy
Singapore 449876 Singapore
**Phone:** +65 6344 4773

#246
## Black & White
Karaoke
**Average price:** Expensive
**District:** Bras Brasah
**Address:** 331 North Bridge Road
Singapore 188720 Singapore
**Phone:** +65 8100 9991

#247
## Molly Roffey's Irish Pub
Pub, Irish, American
**Average price:** Moderate
**District:** City Hall
**Address:** 8 Raffles Avenue
Singapore 039802 Singapore
**Phone:** +65 6238 1875

#248
## The Lilypad
Lounge
**Average price:** Moderate
**District:** Clarke Quay
**Address:** 3A Merchant Court
Singapore 179020 Singapore
**Phone:** +65 6732 3354

#249
## Magic Carpet
Hookah Bar
**Average price:** Expensive
**District:** Arab Street
**Address:** 72 Bussorah Street
Singapore 199485 Singapore
**Phone:** +65 6341 7728

#250
## The Green Door
Bar
**Average price:** Expensive
**District:** Queenstown, Dempsey Hill
**Address:** 13A Dempsey Road
Singapore 247694 Singapore
**Phone:** +65 6476 2922

#251
## Roomful of Blues
Pub
**Average price:** Moderate
**District:** Bencoolen
**Address:** 72 Prinsep St
Singapore 188671 Singapore
**Phone:** +65 6837 0882

#252
## La Viva
Bar
**Average price:** Moderate
**District:** Bras Brasah
**Address:** 01-13 Chijmes
Singapore 187996 Singapore
**Phone:** +65 6339 4290

#253
## Mariko's
Cocktail Bar
**Average price:** Moderate
**District:** Chinatown
**Address:** 4 Jiak Chuan Road
Singapore 089261 Singapore
**Phone:** +65 6221 8262

#254
## O'learys Bar & Grill
Bar
**Average price:** Moderate
**District:** City Hall
**Address:** 30 Raffles Avenue,
#01-04Singapore Flyer
Singapore 039804 Singapore
**Phone:** +65 6337 6718

#255
## Crystabelle KTV Lounge
Art& Entertainment, Karaoke
**Average price:** Moderate
**District:** Chinatown
**Address:** 3 Teo Hong Rd
Singapore 088322 Singapore
**Phone:** +65 6224 7466

#256
## Baden
Bar
**Average price:** Moderate
**District:** Holland Village
**Address:** 42 Lorong Mambong
Holland Village, 277696 Singapore
**Phone:** +65 6463 8127

#257
## TAB
Bar
**Average price:** Moderate
**District:** Newton
**Address:** 442 Orchard Road,
Orchard Hotel, 259800 Singapore
**Phone:** +65 6493 6952

#258
## The Straits Wine Company
Bar
**Average price:** Moderate
**District:** Marine Parade, Katong
**Address:** 180 East Coast Road
Singapore 428886 Singapore
**Phone:** +65 6344 1973

#259
## Harry's Bar
Bar
**Average price:** Moderate
**District:** Raffles Place
**Address:** 30 Robinson Rd
Singapore 048546 Singapore
**Phone:** +65 6324 8076

#260
## Forbidden City/Bar
Bar
**Average price:** Moderate
**District:** Clarke Quay
**Address:** 3a Merchant Court
Singapore 179020 Singapore
**Phone:** +65 6557 6272

#261
## Barber Shop by Timbre
Bar, Pizza, Music Venue
**Average price:** Moderate
**District:** City Hall
**Address:** 1 Old Parliament Lane
Singapore 179429 Singapore
**Phone:** +65 6336 3386

#262
## eM Studio
Bar
**Average price:** Moderate
**District:** Robertson Quay
**Address:** 1 Nanson Rd
Singapore 238909 Singapore
**Phone:** +65 6849 8686

#263
## Sen
Comedy Club, Bar
**Average price:** Moderate
**District:** Geylang
**Address:** 704 Geyland Road
Singapore 389620 Singapore
**Phone:** +65 6841 5653

#264
## Harry's Bar
Bar
**Average price:** Moderate
**District:** Holland Village
**Address:** 27 Lorong Mambong
Singapore 277686 Singapore
**Phone:** +65 6467 4222

#265
## Chamber Food & Entertainment
Pub, Food, Art& Entertainment
**Average price:** Moderate
**District:** Arab Street, Bugis
**Address:** 11 Unity St
Singapore 237995 Singapore
**Phone:** +65 6738 1332

#266
## Woobar
Cocktail Bar
**Average price:** Exclusive
**District:** Sentosa
**Address:** 21 Ocean Way
Singapore 098374 Singapore
**Phone:** +65 6808 7258

#267
## Wine Bos
Wine Bar, American
**Average price:** Moderate
**District:** Arab Street
**Address:** 787 North Bridge Road
Singapore 198755 Singapore
**Phone:** +65 6538 7886

#268
**Molly Roffey's Irish Pub**
Pub, American
**Average price:** Moderate
**District:** Bras Brasah, Dhoby Ghaut
**Address:** 51 Bras Basah Road
Singapore 189554 Singapore
**Phone:** +65 6238 0989

#269
**Robolots**
Bar, Creperies
**Average price:** Moderate
**District:** Joo Chiat
**Address:** 451 Joo Chiat Rd
Singapore 427664 Singapore
**Phone:** +65 6345 0080

#270
**PERFECTO Fusion**
Bar, Asian Fusion
**Average price:** Exclusive
**District:** Raffles Place
**Address:** 3 Pickering Street
Singapore 048660 Singapore
**Phone:** +65 9144 0162

#271
**Harry's**
Bar
**Average price:** Moderate
**District:** Raffles Place
**Address:** 39 Pekin St
Singapore 048600 Singapore
**Phone:** +65 6536 1948

#272
**La Cave Winebar**
Art& Entertainment, Wine & Spirits, Pub
**Average price:** Moderate
**District:** Bras Brasah
**Address:** 30 Victoria St
Singapore 187996 Singapore
**Phone:** +65 6337 9717

#273
**Paradiso Restaurant and Bar**
Bar, Latin American
**Average price:** Moderate
**District:** Sentosa
**Address:** 31 Ocean Way
Singapore 098375 Singapore
**Phone:** +65 6694 5428

#274
**Brewbaker's Kitchen & Bar**
Bar
**Average price:** Moderate
**District:** Sengkang
**Address:** 01-06 Anchorvale
Community Club, 544965 Singapore
**Phone:** +65 6886 1811

#275
**K Union Function Hall**
Karaoke, Venue& Event Spaces
**Average price:** Moderate
**District:** Somerset, Orchard
**Address:** 8 Grange Road
Singapore 239695 Singapore
**Phone:** +65 6756 3113

#276
**Rubato Modern Italian Trattoria**
Pizza, Italian, Wine Bar
**Average price:** Moderate
**District:** Bukit Timah
**Address:** 12 Greenwood Avenue
Singapore 289204 Singapore
**Phone:** +65 6252 3200

#277
**KBox Cineleisure**
Karaoke
**Average price:** Moderate
**District:** Somerset, Orchard
**Address:** 8 Grange Road #08-01
Singapore 239695 Singapore
**Phone:** +65 6756 3113

#278
**The Rupee Room**
Bar
**Average price:** Moderate
**District:** Clarke Quay
**Address:** 01-15 Clarke Quay
Singapore 179021 Singapore
**Phone:** +65 6334 2455

#279
**La Maison Du Whisky**
Bar
**Average price:** Exclusive
**District:** Robertson Quay
**Address:** 80 Mohamed Sultan Rd
Singapore 239013 Singapore
**Phone:** +65 6733 0059

#280
**Lazy Lizard**
Bar
**Average price:** Moderate
**District:** Sixth Avenue, Bukit Timah
**Address:** 2 Sixth Ave
Singapore 276470 Singapore
**Phone:** +65 6468 6289

#281
**Heat Ultralounge**
Bar
**Average price:** Expensive
**District:** Tanglin
**Address:** 2f Royal Plz On Scotts
Singapore 228220 Singapore
**Phone:** +65 6589 7722

#282
## Bernie's Restaurant and Bar
Bar, Burgers
**Average price:** Moderate
**District:** Changi
**Address:** 961a Upper Changi Rd North
Singapore 507663 Singapore
**Phone:** +65 6542 2232

#283
## Nueva Cuba
Bar
**Average price:** Expensive
**District:** Bayfront, Raffles Place
**Address:** 70 Collyer Quay
Singapore 049323 Singapore
**Phone:** +65 6535 0538

#284
## Chameleon Lounge Club
Dance Club, Champagne Bar
**Average price:** Moderate
**District:** Queenstown, Dempsey Hill
**Address:** 22 Dempsey Road
Singapore 249679 Singapore
**Phone:** +65 6479 9929

#285
## The Trenchard Arms
Pub
**Average price:** Moderate
**District:** Joo Chiat, Marine Parade
**Address:** 47 East Coast Rd
Singapore 428767 Singapore
**Phone:** +65 6344 0912

Printed in Great Britain
by Amazon

86008733R00061